MW01014224

HEAVEN ON EARTH, JUST FOR BEING

Light Activation Play-Book

CAMILLE MORITZ
REVELATOR OF LIGHT

BALBOA.
PRESS
A DIVISION OF HAY HOUSE

Balboa Press books may be ordered through booksellers or by contacting:

Balboa Press
A Division of Hay House
1663 Liberty Drive
Bloomington, IN 47403
www.balboapress.com
1 (877) 407-4847

Because of the dynamic nature of the Internet, any web addresses or links contained in this book may have changed since publication and may no longer be valid. The views expressed in this work are solely those of the author and do not necessarily reflect the views of the publisher, and the publisher hereby disclaims any responsibility for them.

The author of this book does not dispense medical advice or prescribe the use of any technique as a form of treatment for physical, emotional, or medical problems without the advice of a physician, either directly or indirectly. The intent of the author is only to offer information of a general nature to help you in your quest for emotional and spiritual well-being. In the event you use any of the information in this book for yourself, which is your constitutional right, the author and the publisher assume no responsibility for your actions.

Any people depicted in stock imagery provided by Thinkstock are models, and such images are being used for illustrative purposes only.
Certain stock imagery © Thinkstock.

Print information available on the last page.

ISBN: 978-1-5043-6616-8 (sc)
ISBN: 978-1-5043-6617-5 (hc)
ISBN: 978-1-5043-6615-1 (e)

Library of Congress Control Number: 2016916179

Balboa Press rev. date: 11/22/2016

CONTENTS

OVERVIEW

My fellow Brothers and Sisters of One-Love.

Heaven on Earth is our Divinely Intended Birthright and Experience.

Humans are not intended to die and leave earth to find or go to Heaven. Humans do not have to prove themselves as worthy to experience Heavenly Life. Death and the worship of death leads to illness, disharmony and lack of freedom. Life and activation of Divinely Intended Life leads to freedom, health, wellness, abundance and joyful purposeful life.

This book is intended to be a model of how to affirm and use the Sacred Power of the Spoken Word to manifest Divinely Ordered Life with ease. The Art of Manifesting is a Sacred Science that has been hidden to protect the Sacred Wisdom during the evolutionary process of humans becoming free, until the Golden Age of Enlightenment is actualized and known through each individuals Sacred-Heart as One-Love. Now is that time, Humans are awakening and each being is naturally becoming heart centered and is now ready to accept the fullness of Life's Sacred Purpose.

This book is a text of Divine Revelation for a time of "The Revealing of Gods Truth". Apocalypse is the Greek word with the definition of revealing divine truth. May it open the seventh seal, bring light and reveal the way for both co-creating and experiencing Heaven on Earth, easily and just for being. Appointed by spirit as a Divine Revelator, I have been asked to share this wisdom. It is now ready to be REVEALED for all who are ready to become heart centered and enter into relationship with self as a sacred worthy being who is originally innocent and a co-creator with Source, choosing Divine Good in every aspect of life.

As a Metaphysical Ascension Manual the information presented is not scientifically proven in this writing. However each reader in highly encouraged to research the concepts through scientific and spiritual resources. Knowledge from outer sources are invaluable for validating inner wisdom and truth of the Sacred Heart Knowing. Each reader is encouraged to learn and use the "Body Pendulum" the "On Board Guidance System" and discern for self the resonation of these sacred concepts through one's own inner sacred-heart knowing and truth.

Many guides through many dimensions have revealed this wisdom and are ready to support, nourish and empower each individual in the transformational process of becoming whole and restoring Peace for, Self, Family, Mother Earth and all sentient beings of earth. Each reader is assured of their belonging as ONE-LOVE, through the Sacred Heart of One, The Law of One. The reader may ask from their own sacred-heart for personal inner guidance and physical demonstration of this guidance in the outer realm.

Master your life or your life will master you. These concepts and practices are the routines and rituals of Spiritual and Self-Mastery. Mother Earth is ascending. (as within so without) All vibrational frequencies are quickening, increasing and activating from within out, either dormant unlimited potentials or hellish life programs. At this time on Mother Earth all unconscious programs, memories, karmic records and hidden agendas are being REVEALED. These may happen blindly through wrath, judgment, injustice, sickness, suffering, war and many other ill maladies in the physical experiences. They may also be transmuted, healed, cleared and unified in Love. Allowing the Individual Being to experience their Unlimited Potentials, Super-Powers and Divinely Intended Abilities as whole, co-creators of Heavenly Life for self and for all unified as ONE-Heart.

This first book of wisdom is the FOUNDATION for our Cosmic Awareness as an Unlimited Eternal Being in Temporary Form. It provides the groundwork for healing the Sacred-Heart, Manifesting Magically and Restoring the Divine Plan of Heaven on Earth. Book Two, will share the process of clearing unconscious programs, akashic records, karmic debt, previous human and non-human lifetimes. Restoring our Divinely Intended Purpose as record keepers unifying all inner strife and wars of separation from with-in out. HEAVEN ON EARTH, JUST FOR BEING. Is our birthright and divinely intended purpose. ETERNAL PEACE, ETERNAL LOVE and OUR INTENDED POWER TO CREATE IT SO. And so it is.

ONLY LOVE IS REAL,

Camille Moritz, Revelator of Light.

CHAPTER 1

Ascension is Now

"There is only One Cast, the Cast of Humanity.
There is only One Religion, the Religion of Love.
There is only One Language, the Language of the Heart.
There is only One God, He is Omnipresent" Sai Baba

ASCENSION IS NOW

Ascension is already happening. All humans on earth are now in the process of readjusting themselves to calibrate with the higher vibrational frequencies of the universe. The vibrational frequency of earth is ascending to a higher frequency. Earth has shifted on her axis and vibrational frequency many times during global events such as earthquakes and tsunamis. NASA has documented 11 earth axis shifts between the year of 1964, and 2013. Earth is vibrating at a faster speed. Ascension of Planet Earth is transformation at a cosmic level. As Planet Earth rises in frequency, so must humans. This process is activating the crystalline consciousness of humanity. Every human's solar light body is now activating and anchoring into physical being. This may be referred to as the Golden Age of Enlightenment.

For humans: Ascension is a Conscious Choice to engage in the natural evolution of life meaning choosing to consciously engage in Enlightenment. Enlightenment can be defined as the state of having knowledge or Divine Understanding. Psychologically enlightenment is the process of self-actualization.

The only constant in life is change. There is a repetitive systematic order to the Universe. Everything is in divine order. Everything is happening on the macro and micro levels simultaneously. Everything has frequency and vibrates. Frequency can be defined as: the rate at which something occurs or is repeated over a particular period of time or in a given sample. It is also the rate at which a vibration occurs that constitutes a wave, either in a material (as in sound waves), or in an electromagnetic field (as in radio waves and light), usually measured per second. Frequencies of our universe are defined and measured with a chart or tool called the Electromagnetic Spectrum. The Electromagnetic Spectrum reveals a repetitive systematic order of the Universe as known by human science. Humans only see a very limited portion of the spectrum experienced as light. Light is individualized through the spectrum of frequencies. When a beam of white light is focused through a crystal prism, the ONE white light individuates into a rainbow of light and 7 visible colors of light emerge out the other end.

This Theosophical systematic order of Light Energy is called Fohat, the divine intelligence and substance of spirit, sometimes referred to as, prana, chi, orgone, universal life-force energy or the higher self. As Light Energy of Divine Intelligence is focused through the evolving crystalline consciousness of the human, the Divine is expressed through Matter on Earth. Humans are both physical matter and spiritual ether. This Divine Intelligence resides as the seed of purity in every particle of matter and in humans. The soul of an individual is the Spirit in physical form. The soul is eternal as spirit is eternal. The form or matter is temporary. Souls carry the records and history of the spirits experience in and out of form.

Part of the Ascension process requires transcending the individual's perception of duality, separation, limitation and global strife from fear based consciousness. This Shift of Consciousness as Christ, Crystalline consciousness happens as the individuals awareness expands from duality into a balanced free will, choosing love through the unified, integrated, awareness of One Universal Heart or Cosmic Consciousness. This awareness is centered in the Sacred Heart Center of each individual. As the frequency of mother earth increases, humans inherently experience expanded states of consciousness through multiple levels of awareness, dimensions and causal bodies. Through Divine Understanding each level of awareness bound to separation and fear based consciousness is now aligned through the one unified heart.

Movement and vibration or a shift in frequency is necessary to clear bound or stuck energetics in a human body. This is the same for Mother Earth. She will shake, quake, erupt, and align her causal bodies with her highest good. Mother Earth is taking back her rightful place as a 5 D planet! It is the divine plan. Volcanoes erupting, weather changes and upheaval are a natural part of this process.

Humans are Angelic Spirit in Physical Form. The Divine Plan is the highest divinely intended idea manifested in physical form. Humans are multi-dimensional Co-Creators of the Divine Plan. Humans are descendants of angels, star brothers, sisters, and earth primates. Each of our ancestral selves must become aligned, unified and fully empowered within and without! All have the power to CHOOSE LOVE IN EVERY EXPERIENCE.

Affirmation: Place Hand on Heart and speak out loud, through the power of the spoken word.

"I take back my power to Choose Love in every experience."
"I Choose Love."

To Know Thyself, is to Know God.

Enlightenment, Ascension, Heaven on Earth.

In the pursuit of Enlightenment and the experience of expanded states of consciousness it is helpful to refer to the historical texts, religious documents, theosophy, theological ideas, theorists and written wisdom available. Each body of knowledge may supply information to assist one in personal process of becoming whole. In some traditions this is the Science of Alchemy, where the individual transforms the lead or lower human consciousness, into the Gold of ascended human consciousness. It is important to measure the resonance or truth of all external information with the inner knowing of the intelligent sacred heart. True wisdom is from the sacred knowing with-in the sacred heart.

In early Ascension Temples such as the Temple or Delphi, people were taught how to gain mastery through the art of "descension". The temple of Delphi had written above its entryway "know thyself". The temple taught the aspirant mastery of the soul's journey or process. This process taught the mastery of descending through the dark underworld of hellish experiences, later to "ascend" into the new life of understanding, and wisdom. Many cultures share mythologies of the three worlds. The over world, underworld and earth world. The Labyrinth is a symbol that teaches the aspirant the transformation process of returning to the center of peace, or the womb of the cosmic mother, center of creation. The 12 labors of Hercules in the Greek myth represent the individual's process of mastery through the Solar Hierarchy.

Through self-mastery one transcends duality and the polarized expressions of duality. The three-fold formulas for transcending duality are keys in becoming individualized. Many cultures have ancient knowledge systems teaching these three-fold formulas.

Wikipedia states that "Theosophy is considered a part of the broader field of esotericism, referring to hidden knowledge or wisdom that offers the individual enlightenment and salvation. The theosophist seeks to understand the mysteries of the universe and the bonds that unite the universe, humanity, and the divine. The goal of theosophy is to explore the origin of divinity and humanity, and the world."

Theosophy from the Greek is the Goddess Theosophia or Sophia, for wisdom or literally "God's wisdom". Theosophy refers to systems of esoteric philosophy concerning, or investigation seeking direct knowledge of, presumed mysteries of being and nature, particularly concerning the nature of divinity. The word "Apocalypse is a Greek word meaning "The Unveiling of Divine Truth". Ascension is the process of unveiling this truth by becoming conscious of one's Multidimensional Being, and unifying each aspect of being.

The following is a list of traditional theosophical concepts considered in the quest of enlightenment.

A list of requirements for ascension includes the following;

1. **Balance 51% of your karma. The Law of Karma states, whatever we measure out to others is measured back to us.** All karma is recorded in the causal bodies of each individual and collectively. The causal bodies are considered to be the Physical, Emotional, Mental, and Etheric bodies. Also called the Memory Body, Astral Body, Desire Body and Etheric Body. Every time we judge ourselves or others, we are karmicly bound to this judgment. By releasing this judgment and reclaiming with intent what we are now choosing to manifest we begin to release and clear these karmic contracts. When these causal bodes are storing more than 51% of an unconscious karmic lesson or experience, it will manifest in physical form through our relationships, life structures and repetitive patterns.

2. **Balance the Souls three-fold-flame in the Sacred Heart.** The three plumes of the Sacred Heart flames are Love, Power and Wisdom. The three-fold flame is the three-fold quality of our divine being. These three-fold qualities are repetitive through-out our multi-dimensional nature and have the attributes of feminine, receptive and having, and of masculine, active and doing, the third attribute is, in the now, knowing as God Goddess in human form. Each of these qualities must be balanced in each of the causal bodies, chakras and multidimensional experiences throughout the souls incarnated history.

3. **Align the four causal or lower bodies.** Each of our lower bodies has a distinct individual experience. They are the Mental, Emotional, Physical and Etheric Bodies or the Memory Body, Astral Body, Desire Body and Etheric Body Often these are in

miss-agreement with each other and each must be aligned with our higher self or our I AM Presence. We than can call forth, I Claim Divine Axiatonal Alignment, asking my Mighty I AM presence to bring each aspect of my being into Divine Alignment with my Higher Self.

4. **Attain mastery of all 7 rays' lessons**, and then learn about the 12 cosmic rays. The seven rays are the seven colors of the rainbow, 7 notes on the music scale and correspond to the 7 chakras. Each has a spiritual lesson, guide, and frequency. Each Ray has an individualized vibration or frequency and must be mastered. Each of the Rays have corresponding angels, guides, totems, etc... Learning which guides work with each of the rays will help one to gain mastery. The rays are not the charkas, but each ray does correspond to a charka in our being. The lessons of the Rays are: Ray 1, Will & Power. Ray 2, Love & Wisdom. Ray 3, Active Intelligence. Ray 4, Harmony through Conflict. Ray 5, Concrete Knowledge & Science, Ray 6, Devotion & Idealism, Ray 7, Ceremonial Order, Ritual and Magic.

5. **Obtain mastery over all outer conditions.** The reality is that ALL IS ONE; there is no separation in Spirit. Each human is free sovereign individualized expression of Spirit in physical form their own color of the rainbow. We need all the colors to form the one white light. Similarly all humans and sentient beings are unified through the one universal heart, of all that is. We must learn to follow our deepest desires from sacred heart with no other person's opinion having matter. It does not matter what any other person says, feels or does, we must be our own Higher-Self in human choosing for our own Highest Good always.

6. **Fulfill ones divine plan.** Each soul has a plan and purpose. Ask your Mighty I AM presence to reveal your plan to you. The Divine Plan is the highest idea or possibility manifested in form. Ones divine plan can be known through the birthright of Divine Revelation.

Affirmation: Place Hand on Heart and speak out loud, through the power of the spoken word. *"I Claim my Birthright to Remember my Original Souls; Origins, Purpose, Mission, Contracts, Lessons, and Intentions. I Claim my Birthright to Remember to Remember".*

7. **Transmute the electronic belt.** The electronic belt is the untransmuted karma that sits in our energetic field around our waist. It is sometimes called the "Dweller on the Threshold" or "Team Dark". It sometimes appears as a dark entity separate from ourselves that tries to keep us stuck in fear. Some experience this as a presence holding them down or back at night. Team Darks essence is all the lower vibrational actions, experiences and unconscious choices of ours souls recorded history.

8. **Raise the Kundalini.** The Kundalini or "Shakti" is the LIFE SOUCE that flow's upwards activating our light body and allowing us to become super human or super spiritual. It is very connected into the Divine Mother or the source of supply from the earth that we lift up to the sky. The Kundalini is the ascension flame. Its purpose to create harmony out of conflict and bring forth order from chaos.

9. **Build the Rainbow Bridge.** Referred to as the Antakarana. A bridge of light built between Personalities, Soul & Monad. Also called the three permanent seed atoms. Its process is to become a human master of form and spirit through alignment of the lower and higher three-fold natures of humans. Unifying the sacred heart of planet earth, human and solar sun. The Antakarana, or Rainbow Bridge, is sometimes called the Tube of Light. Keep a constant 24/7 steady spiraling flow both up and down the column of light.

   RAINBOW BRIDGE INVOCATION: Place your hand on your Sacred Heart and Speak Out Loud, through the Power of the Spoken Word. *I AM the SOUL, I AM LIGHT DIVINE,*

I AM LOVE, I AM WILL, I AM FIXED DESIGN. Repeat invocation daily to build the rainbow bridge.

10. **Activate the Solar Light Body.** Ascension is really a Descension process: the anchoring of the light body, is a process of building our light quotient. The Solar Light Body is the, Mer (light) Ka (spirit) and Ba (body) or Star-Merkaba. It may be referred to as the Diamond Heart, Light Ship, Vortex, Torus or Holy of Holy's. When the fire by friction (internal) merges with electric fire (external) the solar fire, the SOLAR LIGHT BODY is created.

> MEDITATION: (Ascension process) *Imagine being in a **pyramid of light** with the point a foot above the head and the base below the solar plexus chakra.*
>
> *Simultaneously imagine a second pyramid of light with the point a foot below the feet and the base above your heart chakra* (descension process).
>
> Each pyramid is spinning, one clockwise and the other counter-clockwise. These form a Diamond Light Vortex or Torus centered in the Sacred Heart. While centered in the star-merkaba it is a great time to set ones intent and Claim Eternal Peace.
>
> Affirmation: Place Hand on Heart and speak out loud, through the power of the spoken word. *"I Claim Eternal Peace as my Birthright." "I AM at the Center of Peace." "I AM peace." "Only Peace resides in my world".*

"The flute is man, God plays his melody through us" Sai Baba.

LET THERE BE LIGHT.

HEAVEN ON EARTH IS OUR TRUE DIVINELY INTENDED BIRTHRIGHT IN THE NOW.

Humans are creator-beings it is our divine birthright and it is our human-angelic privilege to be the word, eyes, hands and love of God on Earth. When we take back our divine birthrights and claim our power to create, as a God or Goddess or Master in human form, we step into our role to be a co-creator of Heaven on Earth This Sacred Purpose and Process of Co-Creating Hand in Hand with God is our greatest gift and opportunity...

Everything Humans do, think and say is an opportunity to Create Light, Invoke Light, Be Light and Become Light. In its origin the definition of Heaven is thought of as the "Sky Firmament". Firmament also means to "Make Firm or Solid". Human Beings are God Action in Form, the Act of Co-Creation is the process of "to make firm". A Human Being's purpose it to be the ACTION of god, bringing the LIGHT, (chi, fohat, prana, universal life force) into FORM.

"Let there be Light" is an English translation of the Latin phrase FIAT LUX, meaning TO MAKE, or TO DO. "Let there be light", is metaphorically thought of as the spreading of knowledge and the dispelling of wisdom. (Wikipedia) This might also be referred to as Divine Intelligence. Light is both a photon particle and a wave. Light refracts infinitely. Light is measured through its frequency or vibration. Everything known to man as both matter and energy can be measured or identified by its vibrational frequency on the electromagnetic spectrum. Metaphysically there is no difference between Science and Spirit each identifies a systematic order of divine intelligence. (5th ray lesson)

Everything has frequency and vibrates. Frequencies of our universe are defined and measured with a chart or tool called the Electromagnetic Spectrum. The Electromagnetic Spectrum reveals a repetitive systematic order of the Universe as known by human science. Light energy or spirit is individualized through the spectrum of frequencies. The band or spectrum of the Electromagnetic chart that humans can see is the band of Light known as the rainbow. The electromagnetic spectrum contains within it multiple spectrums utilized by humans in science and everyday life a few include, sound, x-rays, sonar, navigation, microwaves, radio waves and telephone waves.

9

Everything is frequency. There is a Systematic order of the Universe.

There are **INFINITE POSSIBLIITIES** for utilizing color, vibration, sound and frequencies for healing activation restoration and balance. The 7 colors of the rainbow, or 7 notes on a music scale, are a band with in a spectrum of frequencies. Each band is a dimension. Each dimension, frequency, color, and sound is an aspect of the Divine and holds within it a seed of purity. Or in other words Its Unlimited Potential.

When a beam of light is focused through a crystal prism, the ONE light individuates into a rainbow of light. 7 visible colors of light emerge out the other end. Just as God individuating through each human as Divine Intelligence. Every hue-man is their own color of the rainbow or an Individuated aspect of Divine Intelligence that is unified as light.

The 7 color rays of the rainbow are red, orange, yellow, green, blue, indigo, and violet. White Light is the unified rainbow or spectrum of Source Energy. The inherent spiritual qualities or virtues of the 7 rainbow colors are:

Ruby Red Ray of the Divine Life Force.
Rose-Orange Ray of Divine Joyful Creative Expression.
Golden Yellow Ray of Divine Illumination, Intelligence and Understanding
Emerald Green Ray of Divine Truth, Science and Healing
Sapphire Blue Ray of Divine Purpose, Will and Devotion
Amethyst Violet Ray of Divine Freedom, Mastery and Transmutation
Sacred White Fire of Purity and Unified Divinity

Divine Intelligence is held within every aspect of sacred life for humans and conspires to continuously communicate in and through humanity through light, frequency, geometry and vibration. Everyday choices of food, surroundings and clothiing, by color, provide the human with natural healing frequencies. Chromo-therapy is the ancient science of healing with color. Each person is already utilizing the natural healing qualities of each ray through the color, sound and vibrations they choose in everyday life. Color is one way of tuning in or being aware of divine guidance. Many times individuals are drawn to a color that provides an empowering healing vibration for that individual. As a conscious tool, each color supplies the body with an intensified frequency or focus as an individuated innate healing quality or virtue of Intelligent Source Energy.

> **Chromo-therapy Charged Color Water Exercise:** Fill a clear or colored glass with water. Place the glass of water on a colored fabric swatch or put colored crystals that are safe to ingest in the glass of water. Place the glass of water with color and healing intent in the sunlight. Let sunlight charge the water for desired amount of time. Usually ten minutes. If you like, tone a frequency or state a verbal decree over the water to add these frequencies. Drink water for integration and healing vibrations of the color attribute.

These seven colors correspond with the seven major chakras, and glands of the body. Light energy or source is individuated through the spectrum of human chakras and organs. Source Energy as Light is taken in through the master pineal gland, and disseminated through each chakra and a corresponding organ of the body. Balance and aligned chakras emit the rainbow colors of the aura. Light Energy or spirit is individualized through this spectrum as the Rainbow Light Body.

An individual's state of consciousness is emitted through the layers of the energetic causal bodies abound the physical body called the aura. Healthy individuals emit a vibrant life force seen as a large colorful aura. Unhealthy individuals emit a smaller, darker and muddier aura. Many intuitively sensitive people see the auric field around people, animals and nature. The colors seen or sensed provide the soul of an individual with innate intuitive information for mastering multidimensional life.

7 Chakra Center Correspondences with color, gland and tones.

Eighth Chakra called the Soul Star, approximately one foot above the crown. Higher-Self, Solar-Heart, Cosmic Gateway transcending duality. May be considered Magenta in color. The color between violet and red.

Crown Chakra	Color Violet	Pineal Gland, Right Brain	Musical Note B. Vowel Sound Ee.
Third Eye Chakra	Color Indigo	Pituitary Gland, Left Brain	Music Note A. Vowel Sound Ay.
Throat Chakra	Color Blue.	Thyroid Gland.	Music Note c. Vowel Sound I.
Heart Chakra.	Color Green.	Thymus Gland.	Music note F. Vowel Sound Ah.
Solar Plexus Chakra.	Color Yellow.	Adrenal Glands.	Music Note B. Vowel Sound Oh.
Sacral Chakra.	Color Orange.	Pancreas Gland.	Music Note D. Vowel Sound Oo.
Root Chakra.	Color Red.	Testes and Overy glands.	Music Note C. Vowel Sound Aw.

Earth Star Chakra aproxamatly one foot below the feet. Eighth Chakra Inner dimentional portal of Earth Heart is activated through balance of three-fold flame of the Sacred Heart. May be considered magenta in color.

Humans are Multi-Dimensional Beings.

Dimensions are octaves or a band within a spectrum of frequencies. Such as the band of light known as the seven colors of the rainbow, or the seven musical notes on a scale of music. Each dimension or Ray is an individuation of an aspect of the divine in frequency called Universal Life Source, Light, Sound, or Fohat.

According to Barbara Hand Clow in her book titled, "Alchemy of Nine Dimensions". Humans must master living in nine dimensions at once. Meaning they must transcend the 8th Chakra into cosmic consciousness of one Global Family of Light. This transition is a Paradigm Shift. Planet Earth is now traveling through the photon band of light called the Galactic Day in both Egyptian and Mayan mythologies that is the time of unified ascension into higher conscious awareness.

Many humans are already living with ease in these dimensions without knowing of this information. It is experienced as a quickening within as each atom begins to vibrate at a higher frequency resonating with the earth's increase in frequency as earth travels through the photon band of galactic light. The Photon Band is an area in space like a band of light. This light is said to come from a central sun, named Alcyone, beyond the earth's sun, in which the Milky Way galaxy revolves. Similar to how our planet revolves around our own sun. Our sun's magnetic flares and geomagnetic storms have steadily increased as our sun entered into this photon band. This period in space has been termed The Golden Age of Enlightenment. This Paradigm Shift is a shift from fear based consciousness to consciousness of abundance and unlimited supply.

In direct light the shadow ceases to exist. In the photon band humanity becomes translucent. All unconscious energetics of both individual and collective shadow are being revealed, revised and transcending into light. **This is a revolutionary awareness in consciousness and a quantum shift in all Ways Means and Measures** that humans have ever known, created and guided each other or themselves by.

According to David Wilcock 35 ancient cultures predicted the earth moving into this Zone of charged planets also called the photon belt. Which would charge up the earth with high solar frequencies. This has been predicted to be a golden age. This phenomena is called "the event" in 2015 social media.

DIMENSIONS:

1 D. Cellular, Minerals, water, genetic codes. Unconscious Mind. Elemental Realm. Atoms or single elements known to humanity through the periodic table of elements. When combined become compounds such as water.

2 D. Biological Matter, Plants, Animals, Lower Brain, Automatic Nervous System, Unconscious Mind. From the center of the earth to the surface, or the center of the atom to the surface of the human body. Referred to as the "Telluric Realm".

3 D. Physical Body, Ego Consciousness, Conscious Mind. The waking and walking experience of life known by humans through time and space.

4 D. Astral Bodies, Higher Human Consciousness, Unconscious Mind. Archetypal patterns played out by humans until the veil or illusionary matrix of limitation is superseded into the conscious awareness of unlimited potential and direct access to source energy through the unified heart.

5 D. Light Body, Unity Consciousness, Super-Conscious Mind. Merging of Spirit and Matter as One through the individual awareness and experience of sacred communion and reverence with all life as One Love. The Spiritualization of Matter.

Multi-Dimensional Chakra System of Infinite Potential

Dr. Joshua Stone of the I Am University teaches a 22 chakra system that helps to understand multidimensionality.

Charkas 1 through 7 are in the 3rd Dimension.
Chakras 8 through 15 are in the 4th Dimension.
Chakras 16 through 22, are in the 5th Dimension.

Each dimension may be thought as an octave of awareness. As the Earth increases frequency, so does the individual. Conscious awareness expands while the light frequencies or codes descend through the human chakra system disseminating Divine Light through the human rainbow body of light and into Earths collective Rainbow Body of Light.

The seven rays individuating through the seven chakras provide guidelines for third dimensional linear time (experienced as time and space) teaching humans the lessons of living as One Human Race through the One Unified Global Heart.

The Eighth Chakra transcends conscious awareness into multidimensional awareness. Universal Consciousness and extrasensory perceptions.

The second set of seven chakras 8-15 begin to descend down through the chakra system until chakra 8 is now below the feet. Then the third set of chakras 16-22 descend down through the chakra system until the individual is fully living in the fourth, fifth, and sixth dimensions through integration of the three-fold nature of being. This in turn activates the Solar Light Body of the individual sometimes referred to as the Star Merkaba. In this system humans are able to continue to expand through the continuous process of enlightenment through the dissension of continuous Divine Light Energies of Source though the Multi-Dimensional Human Vessel of Light.

It may be easier to conceptualize the 22 chakras by thinking about each of the seven chakras having a 3rd, 4th, and 5th dimension within it. Each of the seven chakras has an in breath, an out-breath and the space between. A positive polarity, negative polarity and the transcendence of duality as unified through the Divinely Intended Plan.

Rainbow Prophecy: The Rainbow Prophecy is a prophecy foretelling of an Enlightened Earth where all human and sentient beings are unified through the Universal Heart of One. Many earth peoples, of all colors, and all sentient beings of the cosmos awaken to the awareness of the One Unified All that Is, One Heart of Spirit, One Universal Truth, The One Heart, One Mind, One Tribe, and One Living Planet. The Rainbow Prophecy is a multi-dimensional fable utilizing the rainbow as a teaching system of aligning the multi-dimensional human experiences. Teachings regarding the Rainbow are found in many mystery schools, secret organizations, spiritual mysticism and native lore. A modern day example is that of the masonic adolescent sorority for girls called "Rainbow Girls" which teaches a virtue corresponding to each of the seven rainbow colors.

Other prophetic examples relate similar stories, Such as the Hopi, or Lakota tribes with the prophecy of White Buffalo Calf Woman. The prophecy is that many earth peoples, of all colors and tribes awaken to One Spirit,

One Unified Heart and co-create a world of peace in harmony with mother earth all sentient beings and the universe. Experiencing a consciousness of abundance and an infinite supply of divinely intended resources.

There is a current day phenomena called the "Platinum Babies", where both human babies and animals are being born with platinum or white skin. This phenomena is happening without explanation from genetic science. Whales, tigers, ravens, and moose recently in Alaska are being born white but are not albino. These many white babies both human and animal being born around the earth represent the physical demonstration of the prophecies of ONE as a collective ascension process and a time of great awakening. A time where we give birth to our "Golden Being". Several women have reported they have had the experience of visions and dreams where they are instructed that they will give birth to a Golden Child.

The word Apocalypse comes from Greek language, meaning the "Revealing, Disclosure" or "to take off a Cover". Apocalypse is the first word in the Greek text of the Book of Revelation from the New Testament. The Great Unveiling of Divine Truth is prophesized throughout history and many cultures. Mystery schools have set out to continue the wisdom of this time as a Golden Age where each human and animal rest in peace and harmony. The cultural arts expand and technology serves the Divine Good of Mother Earth.

Source is Light Energy. Humans experience this as Divine Intelligence through both an inner awareness of knowing and an outer awareness of experience. Source as Divine Intelligence is always available to humanity. God, or Source as Divine Guidance is known through inner communion held with-in the Sacred Heart and Mind of Being. Communion with Source is an inherent right and reality of being human. The Sacred Heart is the body space where the mind and heart of God or Source may be known Directly and Personally as Divine Guidance and Understanding.

Spirit Beings or Guides can be thought of as aspects of Divine Intelligence or Light Source identified as ONE God, and perceived by "Hue-Mans" humans through the spectrum of frequencies or 'Hues". "Hues" are the spectrum of colors or frequencies held in the visible band of light. Just as light refracts infinitely creating more light, Source refracts infinitely creating more source.

In many Spiritual Religions and Theosophies, Guides of the Celestial or Heavenly world of Spirit are considered to be of the Angelic Hierarchy. Guides from the Devic or Elemental world of Matter are considered to be the Elohim or Elemental Hierarchy. Humans are the Rainbow Bridge becoming Masters of both Spirit and Form, or Heaven and Earth. Humans Co-Create with and through the Divine Intelligence of God in each sacred aspect of life.

In this same context, the universal life source, or God individuates through each dimension and becomes self-aware in the expanded crystalline, or Christ like consciousness of humans. God is within co-creating with and through each human expression and vibration. Each color, sound, thought, and human is an expression of God. Each human thought, sound, action, and emotion is an expression of god or the light of god focused through the crystalline consciousness and actions of humans. God experiences self through individualized expression of the divine or "those like God" in the selves as Unlimited Understanding and Knowing of Spirit, embodied through the Actualized Heart of the Christ like human who Chooses Right Action aligned with Divine Will. (1rst ray lesson)

Humans who do not choose and are unaware that what they think, say and feel is creating form, are held responsible for every thought, word, and feeling. This responsibility is Karma. The Law of Karma states, whatever we measure out to another or our self, is measured back to us. Choices that are not aligned with the Highest Good of the Divine Plan create life that is less than intended. Humans, who think hellish thoughts, create hellish life. Humans who judge create judgmental life. Humans, who hide, have truth hidden from them. Creations of Humans who create hellish life and experiences without knowing that they did do are call **"miss-qualified Creations"**.

Humans are the creators of Heaven or Hell on Earth, our purpose is To Make or To Do, meaning, we are each the action of God or the universal life energy, incarnated in matter. Humans are multidimensional beings with multiple states of awareness at one time. Our physical body is a denser vibration than our mental body and our emotional body. Humans are the key, the tool, the agent and transducer of universal life force energy. Each of our multidimensional experiences offers the human an opportunity to perceive and experience and an opportunity to choose our perception of each experience. This alchemical process allows Divine Intelligence, God or Spirit to evolve through the human into a Co-Creator Choosing to Create the Divine Plan, or The Highest Good Intended, in each and every experience.

Humans are GODS ACTION in FORM.

> **Affirmation:** Place Hand on Heart and speak out loud, through the power of the spoken word.

> *"I AM the Light of God. I AM the Action of God. I AM the Form or God".*

> *"I AM Gods Action in Form. I AM Gods Light in Action".*

> *"The Light of God is now activated and resides in me and my life".*

> *"The Action of God is now activated and resides in me and my life".*

> *"I AM as God created me. I AM that I AM. I AM Light".*

JUST FOR BEING

EMPOWERMENT, "JUST FOR BEING"

As Empowered Co-Creator Beings, Humans have inherent spiritual birthrights, qualities and virtues. **Inherent** implies our sacred divinity and rights are "**Just for Being**", not for doing. Humans are unlimited beings with unlimited potential. Humans as co-creator beings, are intended to fulfill the Divine Plan of Heaven on Earth The Divine Plan can be thought of as the highest idea, blueprint, possibility or what god would want for each the situation, person, community, planet, universe and the infinite cosmos.

Em-Power-Ment: (three sided triangle)

Em, is to Embody, the reception of divinity and co-creative abilities.

Power, is I AM, Being God Goddess in human form.

Ment, is Intent, the action of the divinity through conscious choice.

Unfortunately, through falling into the illusion of "no choice" many humans have not known the Spiritual Truth of their Unlimited Potential as Co-Creator of the Divine Plan. Many humans are bound to karma through lifetimes of miss-qualified creations, spiritual contracts and vows of suffering, despair and hellish life. Humans have been miss-lead to feel powerless, enslaved and unable to experience a Purposeful Life with Meaning. **Life is Unjust without opportunities.** Divine Justice and Opportunities always come together.

"Heaven has also been defined as an abode for the gods, goddess, angels and those who are good after death." This is not a spiritual truth. It is not our purpose to leave our body to go to heaven; it is our purpose to create heaven on earth through our body.

Hell is defined to be a place of eternal torment in an afterlife, viewed by most as a place of punishment. This is not a spiritual truth. Humans experience hell on earth when they are bound to heaven not being on earth and believe themselves to be less than Inherently Divine. Divine Souls have chosen to incarnate in human form for the mission of co-creating Heaven on Earth through their Sacred Human Body as an alchemical instrument. Whenever conflict resides, the Empowered Human's mission it to co-create Peaceful Harmony. (4th ray lesson) "Out of Chaos, comes Order".

19

Humans have the right to choose in each and every moment. Each choice made is an opportunity to choose for the highest good from the *Sacred Heart.* Conscious Deliberate Intent is the conscious choice to live with deliberate intent from the Divine Understanding and knowing of the Sacred Heart.

Affirmation: Place Hand on Heart and speak out loud, through the power of the spoken word.

"I Claim Freewill and my Power to Choose."

"I Choose to take back my Inherent Divinity, Birthrights, Power and Abilities."

"I open myself to Receive all the Divine Understanding, Abilities and Qualities intended for me."

"I take back my Sacred Power as a Co-Creator, Creating hand in hand with Spirit."

"I Claim Divine Justice and Opportunities as my Birthright."

"I Claim my Sacred Value, Power and Inherent Rights, Just For Being"

It needs to be safe and takes strength for individuals to embody the fullness of their intended power. The consciousness of humans is evolving in waves through "way-showers" who light the way by demonstrating crystalline conscious through being or becoming a Christ in human form. A Christ in human form is an individual who lives through conscious deliberate intent. An individual living with Conscious Deliberate Intent is choosing to live 24 hours a day and 7 days a week as their highest divinely intended self in human form. This individual co-creates with spirit by only choosing in alignment with the one unified good from the sacred heart.

Throughout the history of humanity people have often been persecuted for being different than the norm in their culture. Many souls carry the records of human torture, persecution, cruelty, having no choice and no power. In these experiences of human adversity, the human may only be able to hide or run to keep oneself or family safe. This is especially true of children in our modern day society. Anytime a person has to hide to be safe, that person's soul will bind itself to this frequency and be karmicaly bound to hiding. Each energetic an individual's soul is bound too will manifest in the person's life through the outer experience. Needing to hide to be safe will keep the divine pathway and guidance hidden form the individual bound to hiding. Many times this individual will desire to have the gift of psychic sight called clairvoyance, yet the sight will be hidden due to the hiding contract. Hiding places walls of armor over the heart chakra and over time these walls keep out both the negative and positive life experiences. When an individual has years or lifetimes of heart armor it decreases an individual's intuitive guidance, awareness and trust of self.

Place Hand on Heart and Speak Out Loud: *"I am open to living from my Sacred Heart." "I allow my Sacred Heart to be activated and expand with Unconditional Divine Love and Eternal Forgiveness." I am allowing all heart armor to be dissolved and removed with ease, nourishment and divine timing." "I ask my Higher-Self to remove all heart armor in an easy nourishing way."*

SACRED DOMINION

Our **SACRED DIVINITY** is our **INHERIENT BIRTH RIGHT** and is the **Divinely Intended Plan.** Each Human is a Sacred Worthy Being who has *never done anything wrong and never will!* We are inherently SACRED, worthy and *imperfectly perfect,* **JUST FOR BEING!** We are intended to **LIVE WITH EASE.** Humans are intended to live fully, with Passion, Peace, Joy, Bliss, Purpose and Zeal. **Our SACRED PURPOSE** is to **CO-CREATE HEAVEN ON EARTH** in accompaniment with God's Divine Spiritual Hierarchy. Humans Choosing Divine Good are God's Glorious Form in Physical Expression. Heaven on Earth is the Spiritualization of Matter. All human experiences and soul incarnations are evolutionary opportunities for Spirit to experience a Unique Individualized Expression of matter or God Goddess in Human Form.

God's Fiat: "Man shall have the Gift of Freewill"

As Co-Creator with God, Man has the authority to invoke the presence and service of the Angelic Hosts, which includes the Elohim. Humans have Dominion over the Kingdoms of the Spirit-World and the Spiritual Hierarchy. Humans have FREE-WILL. Angels and Elemental's do not have free-will.

An opportunity has given to the Celestial Kingdom of Angels to receive the Gift of Free Will through the embodiment as a Human Master. Angels incarnating into the world of matter as humans may ascend or evolve becoming Masters of **"As Above, So Below"**. Human Angels who attain mastery as Sovereign Crystalline Beings are Co-Creating the Divine Plan of Heaven on Earth in physical form.

The Seven Archangels correspond with the seven colors of the rainbow. Each Archangel has a twin flame called an Achaia. There is a repetitive pattern of correspondences through the rainbow spectrum of seven, for musical notes, colors, Ascended Masters, Elohim, and Ray Lessons. Every human has 12 legions of angels at their service. Each legion is 144,000. Angels can only assist humans by a human's free will and request for assistance.

The Elohim are of the Elemental Kingdom and do not have free will. The Elementals bind the molecular structure of matter together in physical form. Elementals are in service to God and humanity, they may only ascend through the Sacred-Heart of an Ascended Human Master. The Elohim bring into form and out of form all consciously intended, or miss-intended thoughts, feelings, and words of humans. Elohim exercise this fohatic power to create or UN-create each form.

The twin Elohim Builders of Form hold, bond and bind the molecular structure of the Universe together. The science of Sacred Geometry shows how atoms repeatedly bond and form molecular structures through repetitive geometrical patterns, known as the five Platonic Solids. Each of the platonic solids represents one of five elements. Earth, Air, Water, Fire, and Ether.

Historically Elemental Beings have not had FREE WILL or an opportunity to Ascend through the Sacred Heart as Humans do. They are in service to humanity and bring into form all creations of Humans. Humans are the Sons and Daughters, Gods and Goddess of God, who have Dominion over the Spirit World and are intended to be the Co-Creators of the Divinely Intended Plan or of Heaven on Earth. According to Prophet, Humans have an opportunity to "Command the Life-Essence of Christ to flow to elementals, to infuse them with rejoicing and newness of being and the fire and the spirit to bring the earth into a golden-age".

The Elohim are bound Karmicaly with Humans and carry the heavy burden of poison, toxins pollutions, hardship, lack, trauma, disease, misery and many miss-creations or miss-qualifications of humanity. Through the fall of from Grace, humans have forgotten and have been deprived of the Sacred Truth and Knowledge of Divinity and their true purpose to Co-Create, hand in hand with Spirit.

God's Fiat: is that Man shall have the Gift of Freewill. As Co-Creator with God, Humans have the authority to invoke the presence and service of the Angelic Hosts thereby freeing all elementals in the co-creation of Heaven on Earth.

It is through the Power of the Spoken Word that Mankind is a Co-Creator Being creating Heaven on Earth. The Elohim in service, are then bound through momentum to move out ahead and bring into form the Sacred Word of incarnated God, Goddess or the miss-qualified intentions of incarnated souls yet asleep. **Miss-Qualified Forms** are those in which humans were unaware that what they felt, thought and spoke would bring into form these experiences and actions. Humans are **Karmicaly** responsible for every thought, action and feeling they have. EVERYTHING MATTERS! It is through the Activation of Fohat, the Divine Life Source, and the Sacred White Fire of Purity at the center of every atom that Human Masters are able to restore and co-create the Divine Plan. (When Spirit = Electric Fire) merge with (Living Matter = Fire by Friction) it creates Solar Fire or the Activation of the Solar Light Body! Through this Christ Consciousness Soul and Spirit are unified restoring divine awareness of being Eternal Beings in temporary form. This is the SPIRITUALIZATION OF MATTER. Akash in manifestation expresses itself as fohat or divine energy. Fohat is divine thought or energy (Shakti) as manifested on any plane of the cosmos.

Fohat is the Steed or Electric Life-Force of Source. Also known as DIVINE INTELLIGENCE. Thought is its Rider, Through Conscious Deliberate Choice. Choice=Will.

> *Fohat, is "the animating principle electrifying every atom into life." During the process of manifestation it is the cosmic energy which produces the differentiation of primordial cosmic matter to form the different planes. In the manifested Universe, Fohat is the link between spirit and matter, subject and object. From the Book of Dzyan it is stated: "Fohat is the steed and thought is the rider."*

Place hand on Sacred Heart and speak out loud through the Power of the Spoken Word.

"The Sacred White Fire of Fohat is activated in me and my life."

"The Power of the Divine Life Force is activated in me and my life, to fully restore the Divine Intelligence at the Center of Every Atom of my Sacred Being."

"I AM vibration, I AM energy, I AM light, I AM frequency, I AM fully alive, I AM divine!"

LIGHT ACTIVATION PLAY-SHEET

LIFTING THE VEILS OF ILLUSION AND RESTORING LIGHT.

The Truth See's all and nothing is hidden from Truth.

Twin Flames: Ascended Master Saint Germaine, 7th Ray of Freedom, Mastery and Transformation. Ascended Lady Master Portia, Goddess of Justice and Opportunities, 6th Ray of Peace and Devotion.

Place Hand on Sacred Heart and Speak out loud through the Power of the Spoken Word.

STANDING IN MY DIVINITY AS MY HIGHER-SELF, I send my MIGHTY I AM PRESENCE, out ahead of me to remove all obstacles and fulfill each of these Sacred Decrees, Now fulfilling all Divine Intentions both known and unknown prior to me getting there!

Through the POWER OF THE ONE, UNIFIED HEART, the ONE UNIVERSAL TRUTH, CHRIST ME:

I NOW Acknowledge SOURCE as Infinite Power with-in my Sacred Being. Aligned with Divine Will & Might, I now Claim and take back, ALL the Divinely Intended Power's & Birthright's Spirit intends for me.

I Claim the Path of Overcoming Victory Uniting Higher-Self with Soul. Liberating all aspects of my Sacred Being, I Claim Freedom, Victory and Success for myself and others today and every day!

I Claim FREE WILL and my Birthright to CHOOSE! I Now Choose (24/7) thoughts, behaviors, actions, relationships, locations & experiences that are for my Highest Good, & Highest Joy, as is aligned with Divine Will.

The Divine Action of God Goddess is now Activated and Resides in me & my life to Fulfill all that serves the Highest Good.

There is a Way! I Claim my Birthright to Know the Way, Have the Way and Reveal the Way!

I Stand in my Light, Follow Truth from my Heart, and Hold up my Torch. My Torch Burns through all Obstacles and Lights my Divinely Intended Pathway! ALL IS REVEALED IN THE LIGHT TODAY! ALL IS LIBERRATED IN LIGHT TODAY! Lady Liberty.

I Claim & take back my Sacred DOMINION & Divine Birthright's as Co-Creator of Heaven on Earth.

Through the Power of the ONE I Claim my Highest Divinely Intended, INDIVIDUALIZED Free Sovereign Expression of my God Goddess Self. (I AM the only one...my own color of the rainbow)

Through the Power of the ONE UNIFIED TRUTH OF ALL THAT IS, I Claim and Recognize our One Divine Unified Self as Whole, Sacred, Fulfilled, & Complete. (ALL are ONE)

As Co-Creator walking hand in hand with God, I recognize my sacred purpose to Choose Joyful Loving Life & Desires for the Highest Good aligned with Divine Will from my Sacred Heart. I never need to know how, only the what, or INTENTION. I Decree, and Invoke this desired Intention, releasing it to Spirit... Spirit does the how...I Open myself to receive back to me these divine intentions through Spirit's own Divinely Ordered Form. I thank Spirit for Physically Demonstrating the Way, for each Intention to now manifest, through my own knowing, understanding and through Physical Demonstration.

Divine Intelligence is now activated in me. The Mind of God Goddess now resides in me. I take back my power to think, know and understand as God Goddess. I AM THE DIVINE MIND OF CHRIST!

I Claim Divine Intelligence as my Birthright, taking back my power to KNOW, &UNDERSTAND, as God Goddess does. I now Choose to KNOW, SEE, & ENVISION the Highest Divine Creative Aspect or Virtue for each situation, person, structure, system, or event.

I Choose to Invoke, Command, Proclaim, Decree, Envision, Out-Picture and Speak, These Divine Sacred Aspects & Virtues for myself and all Sentient Beings in every moment hence forth.

The Divine Action of God Goddess now resides in me to BE, DO and FULFILL my Divinely Intended PURPOSE to out-picture, Envision, Act, Create and Empower the intelligence of Christ Consciousness, Buddha Consciousness & Divine Mind in everywhere, everyone & everything!

The Divine Perfection of God's Will is now Activated, Restored & Resides in the Hearts, Minds & Lives of All Sentient Beings. Divine Assurance, Eternal Peace, Safety & Protection is now Activated Restored & Resides in the Hearts, Minds & Lives off All Sentient Beings.

The Sacred White Fire of Divine FOHAT is now activated at the Center of Every Elemental, Celestial, & Human, Sentient or other Dimensional Beings NOW! ALL IS QUICKENED THROUGH THE ASCENSION FLAME NOW!

DIVINE JUSTICE AND LIGHT IS RESTORED, ACTIVATED, & RESIDES IN THE HEARTS, MINDS & FORMS of all Elemental, Celestial, & Human, Sentient or other Dimensional Beings NOW!

DIVINE UNDERSTANDING, ILLUMINATION, INTELLIGENCE, DICERNMENT & KNOWING is Now activated, resides and works through everywhere, everyone, and everything.

DIVINE REVERENCE, COMPASSION, & TOLERANCE for all LIFE, IS NOW ACTIVATED, UNDERSTOOD, and RESIDES in everywhere, everywhere, and everything. ETERNAL FORGIVENESS, PEACE, & ACCEPTANCE is Restored in each Being NOW!

DIVINE HARMONY, CONFIDENCE, & BALANCE IS KNOWN, EXPERIENCED, & RESTORED in the Hearts and Minds of ALL Now.

DIVINE PURPOSE through JOY, & FULFILLMENT, is now, Activated, KNOWN, & Resides in the Hearts, Minds and Lives of All Beings Now!

DAILY I NOW invoke: I SHINE FORTH MY LIGHT, LIGHT, LIGHT, LIGHT, I AM LIGHT! LIGHT IS NOW ACTIVATED IN ME AND MY LIFE! LIGHT IS PRODUCED AT THE CENTER ON MY BONES! LIBHT BURST FORTH FROM EVERY ELECTRON OF MY BEING! I RADIATE LIGHT! I ILLUMINATE LIGHT! I EMANATE LIGHT! I MAGNIFY LIGHT! I AMPLIFY LIGHT! LIGHT, LIGHT, LIGHT, I AM LIGHT! I AM THE LIGHT OF GOD GODDESS! THE LIGHT OF GOD RESIDES IN ME! EVERYWHERE, EVERYONE, and EVERYTHING! LIGHT, LIGHT, LIGHT, I AM LIGHT! OM SHANTI OM......

CHAPTER 2

───────◖▣◗───────

I Am the Light, I Am the Truth, I Am the Way

THERE IS A "WAY"

Stand in Your Light, See Divine Truth, & Create the Way.

"I AM the Light, I AM the Truth, I AM the Way"
Jesus of Sananda, The Wayshower

ALL IS REVEALED IN LIGHT!

Activation of Divine Love and Understanding in the Sacred Heart.

Choose to Light and ignite the spark of divinity in your heart. Imagine a silver cord from your divine spirit or your higher self above your head, a golden sphere of light, coming down into your heart to stay. As your higher-self merges into your heart, your sacred heart flame or spark of divinity is activated and increases. This flame will burn through any anti-light energetic vibration held, until you become one with your higher self. Now you are an empowered radiant being emanating as your highest self on Earth

Divine Revelation is an inherent birthright as a Human Being. It is a system of revealing spiritual truths and answers known through the unified sacred heart. As divine understanding through the balance of Love, Power and Wisdom the threefold flame of being residing in the unified Sacred Heart.

It is through our Sacred Heart we have our God Knowing. The Sacred Heart is our Ascension Chamber, a Star Portal, or the Center of All that Is. It is Zero-Point. Over Millennium humans have been instructed in a miss-truth that the rational mind or intellect is of more importance than our Heart knowing and feeling. That our hearts desires and emotions are week and less than, or that the human body/flesh is sin or a prison.

Humans are co-creator Beings; we are here to be the empowered individualized expressions of our god goddess selves. We are angels in human form and we have dominion over the spirit realm, including both the Angelic and Elemental kingdoms. *"I take back my POWER to be a CO-CREATOR BEING!"*

1. **Place your hand on your heart,**
   a. Placing a Hand on the Heart automatically connects the positive and negative polarities of the mind and heart, much like a battery. The Mind being the place where the First Ray of God anchors, (Will, Power, Purpose, Protection). The Heart being the place where the Second Ray of God anchors (Love and Understanding).

2. Then **Speak OUTLOUD**. We create through the power of the spoken word.
   a. The Throat is the place where the Third Ray of God anchors (Creative Active Intelligence).

3. **Begin to say**, *My Higher-Self now resides in me.*
   a. Imagine a Golden Orb of Light from your God Self or the God Head, descending into the Sacred Heart

4. **Continue speaking out loud** *"Divine Understanding is now activated in me. I Claim my birthright to KNOW, HEAR, and SEE as God Goddess, as Spirit does. I take back my power to Know, See and Hear as God & Goddess does, through my own Sacred Heart, my own Knowing and my own Understanding. I ask my Soul and Higher-Self to be with me today and always. I thank my Soul and Higher-Self for answering all my questions and for showing*

29

me my Divine Pathway. I ask this knowledge and guidance to be **PHYSICALLY DEMONSTRATED, CLEARLY REVEALED, PLACED IN FROM OF ME, I ASK GOD, SPIRIT, and FOR THE BURNING BUSH".**

It is though the anchoring of the Atman, Higher-Self or God-Self in the Sacred Heart that we can know the answers to all our questions and have our Divine Path revealed through us. It is Our Birthright to Know as God does and to be Divinely Guided. When we ask our Higher-Self or God a question from our Sacred Heart an answer is always provided. This answer is in the language of the Soul. The Language of the soul is Symbols, Coincidence, Synchronicity and Metaphor.

> **Place Hand on Heart and Speak Out Loud:** *"I invite my Soul-Self and Higher-Self to be HERE, anchored and activated in my Sacred Heart." "I thank my Higher-Self for clearly revealing Answers, through my own inner guidance, understanding and knowing." "I thank my Higher-Self for divine guidance in every moment from this day forward." "I allow myself to ask source for guidance and to accept this guidance through divine understanding."*

In the beginning it may take several minutes or days for the answer to appear. Usually the answer is something we think of from our inner knowing. It may take time to trust the inner guidance. Each time we trust the message, through aligned intention and action, it becomes easier to trust our inner guidance and knowing. When we experience a coincidence, synchronicity or have an experience of something presenting itself two or three times it is a message of guidance in the language of the soul from our sacred heart knowing. Sometimes animal totems or acts of nature may be messengers. Some may get answers in the dream state at night. When an individual asks the higher self or god from the sacred heart, simply by placing hand on ones chest while asking, an answer is ALWAYS returned. Trusting and understanding is a process that becomes easier with practice.

The answers are returned to us through the language of the soul. The Language of the soul is symbolism, color, coincidences, synchronicity, metaphors and extra sensory intuitive awareness's through the five primary senses. The five primary senses in the heightened awareness's are the individuals intuitive "SUPERPOWERS" and allow one to experience heightened awareness, guidance and fulfillment. Each body of knowledge an individual learns or has awareness about, will be picked up by the higher-self and delivered back to the individual through heightened awareness's of the senses. Knowledge may be thought of as a body of information we learn from outside or external sources. Wisdom may be thought of as inner guidance aligned with the unified good through discernment and balance. It is important to always score, or sense the resonance of outer knowledge with the knowing truth of the sacred heart. This may be done through the **"On Board Guidance System"** of the Sacred Heart, referred to as the **Body Pendulum.** Each extrasensory awareness and individual experiences can be confirmed or validated through the body pendulum in the sacred heart. Some individuals become adept in kinesiology or muscle-testing; these skilled abilities allow for very clear divine guidance and are recommended studies.

Example: A medical intuitive may have spent many hours studying the human anatomy. As a result when the medical intuitive scans an individual, Spirit Knowing delivers this information back to the medical intuitive through seeing, knowing, feeling, the body of knowledge studied. Another example is being guided through hearing a song that one may have heard on the radio waves. A third example is seeing a tarot or oracle card prior to laying out the cards and without having any cards present, as a way for spirit to deliver information.

The Five Extra-Sensory Perceptions:

As the individual begins to tune into divine guidance through the sacred heart knowing, Source as Higher-Self, or Atman takes an interest in the human by "Putting Down" guidance or information that demonstrates to the individual the Way or Answers asked from the Sacred Heart. Divine Guidance is delivered through the human who is open to receiving information. This guidance is always delivered through the language of the Soul which is metaphor, symbolism, coincidence, and synchronicity and through the newly heightened five extra-sensory perceptions.

The five extra-sensory perceptions are channels allowing Higher-Self and Soul to communicate in and through each individual. It is imperative that each individual become self-empowered with self-mastery of the human body temple as a Vessel of Source. The human must master the vehicle or human vessel by taking Dominion of Self as a free Sovereign Being. The Body is a Divine Temple for co-creating the divine blueprint into form. If the Human does not take dominion of self, the body becomes a vehicle for low vibrating entities and unconscious energetics to reside within and work through. Thus creating chaos, disorder and hellish life for self and many. Traumatic experiences, wounds with trust, soul level contracts, karmic agreements, unconscious emotions, attachments, past and current cognitions may inhibit all the extrasensory abilities.

Claiming Sacred Dominion as a Free Sovereign Being and clearing the vessel of inhibiting energetics will free the individual and strengthen their Divinely Intended Intuitive Abilities. Activating the Unlimited Potentials, in the human DNA will activate the extrasensory intuitive channels as Humans Super-Powers.

Clairalience: or Clear Smelling is the phenomenon of smelling spirit, guidance or those who have passed over. Many times the Spirit of Divine Mother is experienced through the fragrant smell of roses or flowers. Loved ones who have passed may be experienced as smoke, perfume, baby powder or food. Usually the odor is similar to the smells around the loved one prior to their passing.

"The nose always knows" the olfactory system has only one neuro-synapse between the nose and the pituitary gland. Smelling is a powerful way of healing primal trauma. Through Aromatherapy the soul is quickly able to heal and restore the unlimited self. The nose as a primal sense of protection may be heightened in smelling future dangers, upcoming weather, storms or other awareness's.

This sense may be blocked and shut down through soul level contracts and the energetic records of trauma. Trauma from previous wounds in the head or nose area. Trauma associated with smells. Smells at the time of death in previous lifetimes. Such as having a past life where one died in a battle field of roman chamomile. Then in this life the smell of roman chamomile might be repulsive for that individual without having a rational understanding of this awareness. Sometimes people will manifest allergies as a result of stored energetic traumas or agreements. A childhood experience of being exposed to cigarette smoke without an opportunity to leave is another example of when the sense of smell might be energetically blocked or shut down as an adult.

The extrasensory olfactory sense may also bring to the individual unwanted smells such as excrement. Low vibrating entities such as the shit demon may be experienced as the smell of feces. This often occurs where entities or demonic possessions may be experienced. Sometimes this is in connection with the death wound of crucifixions or disembowelments where hundreds of bodies who were tortured released excrement on earth soil. The smell of psychic excrement is also an indicator of being bound or obligated to take care of other people's shit or karmic debt.

> *Thank you Higher-Self for the activation of my Divinely Intended Smell. I claim and take back my inherent right and reality to smell as God Goddess smells. Divine Smelling is now activated in me and in my life.*

> *I claim my inherent right to Know through my nose, with ease just for being.*

> *I claim the power of my divinely intended smell.*

Clairgustance: is Clear Taste, without putting anything physically in the mouth. This is similar to smell and is commonly paired with smell. This sense sometimes may be used to deliver messages about safety like poison verses pure substances. An example is the intuitive statement that something experienced, "leaves a bad taste in my mouth".

The extrasensory ability of clear taste may be shut down and inhibited through energetic agreements, and past traumatic experiences. If clairalience or clear smell is inhibited then the sense of taste may also be in habited.

> *Thank you Higher-Self for the activation of my Divinely Intended Taste. I claim and take back my inherent right and reality to Taste as God Goddess smells. Divine Tasting is now activated in me and in my life, with ease just for being.*

> *I claim the power of my divinely intended taste.*

Clairaudience: is Clear Hearing of music, sound, and thought form's from another dimension. This may be experienced through the hearing of music, messages or guidance from inner sound or voice. It is considered a form of channeling. Many times messages are delivered through current day music or the music of a passed over loved one. Inner Hearing is common for many. I hear music every morning as guidance from higher-self. Higher-Self utilizes the inner voice to give direction and guidance.

The extrasensory sense of sound or hearing may be blocked, inhibited, or shut down where sound is paired with trauma, through previous child or past life experiences of having no ability to shut out parental arguments or other disturbing sounds. Conscious language of self or others may inhibit the senses as well. Such as a child always hearing from a parent, shut up or be quiet, later this will be replayed though the individual's own inner hearing. An another example where inner sound may be blocked is when an individual makes an energetic agreement to not speak or express one's own truth to keep the self-safe. Cultural clichés are often clues as where a sense may be inhibited. Such as the saying "children are to be seen but not to be heard, or no one ever listens to me"

If the human has not taken dominion of the sense of hearing, the human may experience hearing one or many voices shouting, cursing of giving the self, negative directions. Un-transmuted karma known as the "dweller on the threshold" or "guardian at the gate" may take over the inner hearing and be experienced as demonic voices, unwanted orders or repetitive thought forms that are self-detrimental such as thoughts of suicidal or homicidal ideations.

Many humans have implanted "recorders" at the base of the skull and wrap up around the ears and sometimes down the spine. They replay negative or false thought forms and give destructive directions to limit the individual. The recorders were implanted by controllers of the archonic dimensions and are activated in humans during the ascension process to limit the human from direct access to the divinely intended source energies. These can be easily deactivated as the human begins to claim free will and unlimited access to source energy as divinely intended through the One Unified Heart.

Sometimes what an individual's hears in spirit is difficult to speak out loud. One may be hearing in one dimension and trying to repeat what was heard in another or lower dimension. Through conscious choice, development and request of Higher Self this process will become easier.

> *Thank you Higher-Self for the activation of my Divinely Intended Inner Sound and Inner Hearing. I claim and take back my inherent right and reality to hear as God Goddess hears. Divine Hearing is now activated and restored in me and my life.*

> *I claim my inherent right to express my voice and truth with ease, just for being.*

> *Thank you Higher-Self for the easy ability to hear intuitively and share this knowing in voice and cognitive expressions.*

> *I claim the power of my divinely intended sound, frequency and voice.*

> *I AM the voice of God Goddess.*

Clairsentience: is Clear Feeling or Psychic Sensing, of other realities or entities through the sense of touch. It is empathic and kinesthetic in nature. It is sensing information through the physical body. Some common experiences of clairsentience include, tickling sensations, hairs on the back

standing on end, and shivers through the body. As an intuitive
matic sensations may show the intuitive a client's illness, ailments
paces to address.

Clarisentience is inhibited and shut down in physical and sexual trauma.
Distrust of the mother or trauma with the mother keeps the self from
trusting this empathic body sense. Because the body or matter is feminine
in its alchemical nature.

This empathic sense may be heightened to a self-detriment in manifesting
as hypersensitivity, anxiety, phobias and hypervigilance. The empathic
sense may be withdrawn or limited in trauma if the human withdraws
their life energy by residing above the body verses in the body. The body
may become filled with other people's energies, psychic chords, entities,
and karmic obligations keeping one from being able to discern if the
empathic energy sensed is the self's or is another individuals or a group of
individuals. If the empathic self is not mastered it becomes the body of pain
that is rejected, denied, overemphasized and may rule our physiological
experiences.

> *Thank you Higher-Self for the activation of my Divinely Intended
> Empathic Abilities.*
>
> *I claim and take back my inherent right and reality to feel as God
> Goddess Feels. Divine Sensing is now activated and restored in me
> and my life.*
>
> *I am now the only thinker in my head and the only feeler in my body.
> I am no longer willing to carry others energetics or pain in my body.*
>
> *My body is a vessel of Light, Only God Light resides in me and works
> through me.*
>
> *Through the power of source in my sacred heart I am a healing vessel
> of love, light, truth, peace and divine order.*

Claricognizance: is Clear Knowing, a direct sense of knowing an answer or information. An example is knowing the answer to a math formula without doing the math. It is an automatic sense of wisdom or information known from within, without seeking the information from the outer world.

Distrust of the father may inhibit knowing because the mind is spirit or masculine in its alchemical nature. Distrust of the father may also be distrust of god or source and experienced as separation from divine guidance. Verbal statements such as "I don't know" will block clear-knowing. Soul agreements and contracts that limit the self, such as a person hiding their intelligence may inhibit the sense of Clear-Knowing.

Direct knowing is considered a direct channel to source energy. It may be experienced as an "AHA" thought. The individual may dismisses it as a fleeting thought verses knowing the energy is directly put down by Source or Higher-Self to guide the self.

> *Thank you Higher-Self for the activation and restoration of my Divinely Intended Knowing as Clear Cognition.*

> *I claim and take back my inherent right and reality to Know as God Goddess hears.*

> *I AM the Divine Knowing of God Goddess. I know as god knows. God knows through me. I am the cognitions and thoughts of Source Energy.*

Clairvoyance: is Clear Sight and 'seeing' beyond the five senses. It is experienced as seeing guidance through the inner eye in visions, images, pictures, symbols, and geometrics.

Clear Inner Sight is activated through the process of visualization and imagination. Bodies of knowledge and information that are studied and learned may be returned to the individual intuitively through inner sight. An example is learning the physiology of the human body then later seeing a muscle or inner body space as guidance for restoration of health.

This sight will give the individual answers and solutions when activated as divine revelation.

Clairvoyance may be experienced as a vision or seeing possible future events. Clairvoyance may have sight of the past, present or future circumstances. As a protective defense clairvoyant knowing may predict a future event allowing the individual to choose an alternative path and create a new safe outcome.

The clairvoyant sight is also a channel for seeing into other dimensions known by some as the spirt world. This sight may see the aura or causal light bodies around humans, plants and animals. One may see beings from other realms, such as angels, ascended masters, magical beings, and ghosts, extraterrestrial's, entities and many more.

A person's emotional state and level of conscious awareness will be reflected in ones Divine Sight. Fear of seeing will prevent intuitive sight. Past traumatic experiences, withdrawing ones energy, soul contracts of blindness and hiding block and inhibit clairvoyance.

Many humans have "blinders" in the frontal or temporal lobes that are implanted by controllers of the archonic dimensions and activated during the ascension process to limit the human from direct access to the divinely intended source energies. These can be easily deactivated as the human begins to claim free will and unlimited access to source energy as divinely intended through the One Unified Heart.

Thank you Higher-Self for the activation and restoration of my Divinely Intended Clairvoyance.

I claim and take back my inherent right and reality to See God Goddess Sees.

I AM the Sight of God Goddess. I see God, God sees me.

I Claim the Power of my Divinely Intended Sight.

Place Hand on Sacred Heart and Speak out Loud,

Divine Solutions and Answers are revealed to me with ease, just for being.

"I Claim my Divine Sensory abilities. I take back my divine right to Smell, Hear, See, Taste, Know and Understand as Divinely Intended."

"I Claim my Divinely Intended Super Powers of Extra-Sensory Perception, with ease, just for being."

Each of the humans senses become more refined through increased conscious awareness and clearing the unconscious energetics binding one to limitation. At first the human's extrasensory intuitive abilities are instinctual and heightened or activated in danger. Eventually the extrasensory senses become channels of intuitive guidance and the superpowers of multi-dimensional being.

BEING YOUR DIVINELY INTENDED SELF.

EEE, EQUAL EXCHANGE OF ENERGEY.

Divinely Intended Relationships have the Divine Qualities and Virtues of God Goddess in an *equal exchange of energy* as Divine Fellowship. Where each person recognizes, inspires and empowers a fellow brother or sister as a Sacred Being who is becoming a Walking Christ. Lifting each other up through unconditional love, acceptance, kindness and compassion. Each relationship is intended to have an *Equal Exchange of Energy.* This begins in the conscious recognition that each person is an Individualized aspect of the Divine. Each person is co-creator who is inherently worthy and sacred. Just for Being.

> *"I open myself to experience, understand and be conscious of having an Equal Exchange of Energy in my relationships with life, with god, with humans and with other beings."*

In the process of healing the Sacred Heart, the individual begins to restore Sacred Trust through healing wounds of the three-fold heart flames.

Sacred Trust is restored when the heart flames, Power, Love and Wisdom are healed in all relationship experiences. These are the soul wounds held between the child and mother or father. Held between woman and man or brother and sister. All karmic life experiences as either a boy, girl, man, or women that are less than intended are a betrayal of Divinely Intended Life causing the soul to withdraw, shrink and misconstrue Sacred Life, Sacred Relationship and Sacred Living.

Relationships allow the soul to experience a spectrum of individuality and separation from one source. The individual's relationships and outer life mirror back to the soul, all unconscious programs, wounds, contracts, curses, misaims and karmic blockages.

Consciously aware individuals may choose to explore, know, love and heal the shadow or unconscious self, by recognizing that every relationship is a mirror of self. Every outer experience in the individual's life is a manifestation of the unconscious self or of the individual's resonant frequency. All outer experiences are *Maya* a holographic illusion allowing the soul to evolve into the Divinely Intended Plan of Co-Creating Heaven on Earth.

Each experience in life with another is NOT PERSONAL. If it feels personal, and has an emotional charge, it is Karmic. Meaning the soul is storing an unconscious energetic that is playing out in this outer reality or relationship experience to give the soul the choice, freedom, information and ability to now release and clear the energetic or karmic record.

This process may be called Soul Transformational Work or Processing. I refer to this process as *Stepping off the Wheel of Karma*. Meaning the individual is now taking responsibility for all outer experiences as an extension of self/source. The forward momentum of the unconscious programs or energetics as karmic patterns will no longer roll over the individual as an illusionary duality. Instead the individual begins to utilize the Sacred Science of Manifestation as an Empowered Co-Creator Being to imprint the universe and outer reality. This process raises the individual's resonant frequency. Thus the outer environment, life and relationships must now match the individual's new frequencies, intentions and choices.

Each frequency can be measured and expressed through mathematical numbers or equations. Each number is a frequency and has a state of being. In esoteric systems and Soul Transformational Work the Divinely Intended Blueprint is the pure full potential of matter. It is the Archetype, Blueprint or Divine Idea that is evolving through each being. Each number is a reflection of this state of being and has a soul lesson or identity that each human is processing, projecting, experiencing and creating. For the number ONE the experience or lesson is unity, individuation and being source. For the number Two, the experience or lesson is RELATIONSHIP or duality. The self and others. The self and God. The self and everything else. This is the experience of Duality and Separation. Being separate from God, the mother, father, abundance, love or other divinely intended sacred heart needs. Yet it is through duality that the human is able to become aware of individuality, personal power and sacred purpose.

The self is sacred and relationship is sacred. The souls true purpose is to love self, others, source and all life as ONE in every experience no matter how perceived by the lower mind or by other people's opinions. As conscious awareness expands the individual soul naturally loses the perception of being separate from source. The soul is storing the records as programs, yet the spirit always knows the TRUE DIVINELY INTENDED and is continuously evolving to BEING as Divinely Intended.

"I AM AS GOD CREATED ME".

Heart Centered Awareness expands into cosmic awareness of being unified. As one global consciousness, one cosmic consciousness and One Unified Sacred Heart. (EARTH=HEART) In higher states of awareness the human soul loses perception of being separate from other humans as we are ONE Source. *It is through the Law of One that humans are intended to be Free Individualized Aspects of One Unified Source.*

SACRED RELATIONSHIPS.

In the spiritual lessen of the ONE humans become conscious and aware of existing and being alive. Through the power of the ONE humans are unified as Source Energy. Humans have choice and free-will. Through conscious awareness an individual can choose to be the Divinely Intended Self as an eternal being in temporary human form. This is the awareness of I AM or, I AM that I AM.

When the human moves into the vibration of the ELEVEN, or TWO, they step into the lesson of SACRED TRUST. (11= 1+1=2) Becoming aware of Unity and Separation with Source or God. With self and with others as relationship. Are we separate from God, and our family, or are we unified with them.

(11:11 = Divinely Intended Blueprint, DNA Light Activation = Sacred relationship with self. Sacred relationship with God. Sacred relationship in Divine Partnership. Twin-Flame Relationships. The Sacred Marriage. Heaven on Earth.)

The human awareness of duality allows the individual to experience their own unique individualized God Goddess Self as an individualized aspect of source or an Eternal Being in temporary human form. This is a relationship based on sacred trust. The soul wound of separation keeps the human from the experience of belonging and being supported by other humans and by Source.

The awareness of separation may cause pain and disconnection from the divine self. When humans experience separation from others they begin to experience and perceive relationships as less than divinely intended. Leading one to question the trust of God and others?

1. What is my relationship with God or Spirit?
2. What is my relationship with myself?
3. What is my relationship with my friends, family, lover, community, and the world?

One may need to reclaim the DIVINELY INTENDED SELF, to step into the new paradigm of higher vibrational frequencies. To do this one must release dense, outdated, previously made belief-systems regarding relationships with Spirit, Ourselves and Each Other. I have found it quite helpful to follow this procedure to do this.

1. *Higher-Self, God, Source, I release, (hand to you) any beliefs, ideas, thoughts, routines, structures, that I have or hold about what or who you are. These include all that are either conscious or unconscious. I give these freely to you. I open myself to receive who God, Source, or Spirit back to me through my own divine understanding as Divinely Intended.*

2. *Higher-Self, God, Source, I give myself to you, any way I have ever thought about myself, or felt about myself. Any way I have judged myself, believed myself to be, or expected of myself. Any role I have placed myself in. Anyway I have ever known myself to be, I now give to you freely. I open myself to receive who I am back to me through Gods will, in my highest divinely intended form. This is being anchored into my heart, life, knowing and divine understanding.*

Originally Innocent.
"I claim my original sacred innocence and ask it to be activated in me and my life, in the now with ease just for being."

Be open to seeing and experiencing self as divine, worthy, sacred and valued. Be open to accepting self as a divinely intended being who has never done anything wrong and never will. A being whose worthiness and sacred value is just for incarnating into human form.

3. *Higher-Self, God, Source I give this person to you, anyway I have ever thought about him, known of him, expected of him, desired of them, judged them, wanted from him, or limited them, Any preconceived role I have placed this person in. I give everything about this person to Spirit freely.*

If this relationship is no longer for my highest good, I know Source will do its perfect work to shift this relationship out of my path, If this relationship is for my highest good, I know Source will do its perfect work to remove all obstacles and clear the path for this relationship to be brought forth in its highest form.

I now open myself to receive this relationship back to me through its highest form. In Gods own divinely ordered way. Through Spirits divine will, love, and understanding. Which is now being anchored into my own heart, knowing, life and understanding. I open myself to receive the love that this person has not the love that I want. (The love that I want from others I now do for myself)

SACRED TRUST.

Sacred Trust is restored as the individual becomes open to accepting and recognizing the self as Sacred Source. As a valuable being who is inherently worthy and divine just for being. For incarnating into human form. Trust in Source, Trust in humans, Trust in Self, and Trust in the process of becoming light all increase through setting the intention and claiming to have Sacred Trustworthy Life and Relationships.

"I Claim Sacred Trust as my inherent right and reality. I now only draw to me Trustworthy Life, Trustworthy relationships, people, situations and events. Sacred Trust is Now Restored in my Life, with ease, just for being."

"I open myself to experience trustworthy life, trustworthy relationships and trustworthy solutions for my divinely intended sacred heart needs. Thank you, higher-self, thankyou God for the Sacred Experience of Sacred Trust and Sacred Relationships in the Now, Easily and Just for Being."

ONLY LOVE IS REAL.

I am the light, I am the truth, I am the way.

I AM THE LIGHT.

1. Choose.

"I choose to stand in my light!" Only you can choose to stand in your light. Your light is your divinity; it is your birthright to be a co-creator of heaven on earth. It is your birthright to claim your divinity. Each time you claim your birthright to stand in your light, you light the way for your freedom. When standing in our light all darkness, unknowing, and fear falls away. Standing in one's light brings clarity, joy, illumination, light heartedness, a lighter body, and lights the way for us to know and understand truth. Choosing to stand in your light also begins the process of anchoring the light-body into the physical body. It is your light-body and it is safe to be a Being of Light on Earth.

> **Place Hand on Heart and Speak Out Loud:** *"I choose to stand in my light!"*
>
> *"I take back my divinely intended power to stand in my Light"*
>
> *"I release all agreements I have ever made in any life time human and non-human that I must hide to be safe. I take back my power to stand in my light, freely, easily and safely."*
>
> *"I claim my Divinely Intended Birthright to be Safe and Protected, with ease, Just for Being!"*
>
> *"I now only draw to me; life, people, situations and events that are Safe and where I am Safe and Protected." "I Claim Safety as my Birthright." "All is now Safe in my world."*
>
> *"I release all Hiding Contracts!" "I take back my intended power to co-create a new reality, I now choose to create life where it is safe to be light, have light and stand in my light. I choose to create life where*

45

it is safe to exist and take up space. I choose to create life where it is safe to speak out lout, to be loud to make noise and speak truth. "I Choose to create life where I AM safe to Stand! I stand in my Truth, I stand in my Light, and I stand for myself, freely easily and safely, With Ease, Just for Being!"

"I Stand in my Light, I follow truth from my Sacred Heart, I hold up my Torch. My torch burns through all obstacles and Lights my Divine Path Way!" Lady Liberty....

"I AM open to having all heart armor and defensive energetic patterns removed, in an easy, safe nourishing way." "I Claim Divine Safety in being Open Hearted and living from my Sacred Heart."

"I thank the Spirit and the Angels for fulfilling each of these sacred decrees from my sacred heart for me now and I thank Spirit and the Angels for physically demonstrating to me this fulfillment through my own understanding and awareness."

2. Initiation, Gaining Mastery. Every experience is an opportunity to Choose Again.

Initiation refers to a space of limbo or void. It is the space between the individual soul being bound to the old energetic matrix and the new energetic matrix, through divinely aligned conscious choice manifesting into physical form. Initiation is implied to an "initiate" meaning an individual or student gaining mastery through freewill and repetitive practice until the desired conscious choice is fulfilled. In theosophy the term Aspirant referred to as an individual on the aspiring path towards enlightenment.

When we are initiated, it feels like being tested. It may be necessary to choose to be your empowered light self at least three or more times. When we choose to stand in our light, we begin to face what is traditionally known as the "Dweller at the Threshold", or the "Guardian at the Gate". Today I refer to the dweller or guardian as "Team Dark". This is a term applied to all of our previously created structure, and karma that limits our ability to be our highest self in the now. In our personal history of this lifetime or our soul's history of past lifetimes, we have created many limitations for ourselves. An example of this is if you have ever said, "I don't understand", these words and thoughts have gone out ahead of you and have created more not understanding in your life, or when you stated something was hard, you then created more "hardness" in your life. Another example is if you have experienced getting in trouble for knowing truth or being seen, you may have stated that it is necessary to hide, or not be seen, in order to be safe. As you may already know, every thought is a thing and creates what it is in physical form. Every word goes out ahead of us and creates what it is in physical form. So every time you have declared you are trapped, bound, powerless, etc. you have then created this experience even more for yourself. The Guardian at the Gate, has sometimes been referred to as our shadow self. Our Shadow Self is all we have pushed away, denied and judged of self. Team Dark, will sometimes show itself as a demon, or a dark figure. We may see Team Dark as an oppressive being in our dreams, visions, or energetic work. When you begin to claim your divine right to be a creator being of light, it will be necessary to confront the shadow self, inviting all history of playing the role of team dark or team light into the one heart of love. First we must have compassion and love for our shadow self; after all it has served us perfectly by protecting us and keeping us safe. Team Dark has really been our ally; it was created in the absence of love and divine understanding. When we thank the Team Dark and invite it into love, it immediately allows this shadow self to be transformed into its higher form by becoming a part of our empowered self. This process may not seem that easy. However, remember it is your birthright to experience love, light, peace, and abundance, so begin today to take back your dominion and power to be a co-creator being of heaven on earth.

Think about all previous individual karma being a big wheel, like a giant snowball that is rolling over the top of you. The snow ball was built through the soul binding itself to beliefs and self-governing structures that are not aligned with the unified good from the sacred heart. This wheel of karma, has forward momentum and takes time to stop rolling. As the individual stops feeding the wheel with repetitive patterns and miss-aligned choices, the karmic momentum or wheel diminishes and melts away. As the individual Soul begins to build a new momentum through conscious deliberate intent the individual's world is now experienced and manifested into form from these conscious choices and the new repetitive forward momentum is created. *To out-picture is to envision a sacred intent as if complete and fulfilled in the now, until it does manifest in physical form.*

As an individual begins to affirm new life choices the unconscious energetics one was bound to from the past will come to the surface of awareness through the outer experience and such as in the environment or relationships. This has been referred to as projection. Unconscious energetics may also be experienced somatically through body symptoms and pains. These are the unknown unwanted aspects in shadow self or our own personal team dark. In a world of duality team dark and team light may be experienced as polarized opposites. The polarization is what puts a karmic "charge" on the experience and its own forward momentum.

The path of mastery and enlightenment involves loving every aspect of team dark and team light through the unified balanced heart of Christ Consciousness. Each human experience is sacred and AN OPPORTUNITY TO CHOOSE AGAIN. Light is Sacred and Dark is Sacred.

Place Hand on Heart and Speak Out Loud:

"I invite all fear and lower emotions into love, thanking the angels for escorting them there."

"I take back my power to Choose Again." "I Choose a new reality aligned with my divine good from my sacred heart."

"I now choose to pair all negative low vibrating thoughts with the highest intended idea and speak through the power of the spoken word, the new chosen thoughts into form."

"I invite all fear of voicing my sacred decrees, into love."

As Above So Below,

Everything known to us as Heaven or Nirvana is really intended to be in form on earth. In fact the microcosm is a reflection of the macrocosm and vice versa. As Above So Below refers to what we know of as the divinely intended or heaven from our sacred heart. So below refers to the macrocosm is a mirror and repeat of the microcosm.

As With-In So With-Out,

All the sacred desires we store in our sacred heart are intended to be in form in our outer world. In fact every unconscious energetic we have stored in our records is a magnet drawing to us the mirror of it in our physical experiences.

Shifting the 8 to the Infinite....

Heaven is not intended to be above Earth or outside of our human experience. In fact we are multidimensional beings experiencing the sum result of our previous vibrational frequencies and we are co-creator beings choosing to create the New Life in a Paradigm Shift.

We are both Spirit and Human. We are Human Angels, God's and Goddesses in a human form. Both are Sacred! Light is sacred, dark is sacred. All dualities are but the same, Individuation, In Divinity, Indivisible, and Unified as one whole being of sacred intent. We exhale, and inhale, contract, and expand, we experience separateness and sameness, unity and division. Both Are Sacred!

All of our beings experiences and sensations serve us perfectly, each designed to teach us and give us opportunity to stand in our birthright to choose. We have Free Will, We can choose. "I choose to stand in my Light", "I choose to Love", "I Choose Truth", "I choose to Forgive".

As Humans *choosing* to be our highest self, our God/Goddess Self, we sometimes begin to think of our Human experience as less than our God/Goddess experience. However Both are Sacred!

As Humans experiencing duality, and multidimensionality, we sometimes begin to judge parts of our experience as being better than other parts. Our human mind or intellect as being stronger or better than our human emotions. Our self- governing structure and desire to control as being better than our flexibility or ability to let go. Our physical body as being less than our Spirit or Divine Self. As we play this game with ourselves, we begin to deny the "less than experiences" by pushing them into the shadow part of our being. Our less than experiences, such as fear and cruelty have never known love, for they were created in the absence of love, they remain in the shadow of denial and human judgment. Releasing all judgment of our 'less than experiences' frees them. Loving our "less than experiences" heals them. Inviting fear into love, allows it to heal and be brought forth into its highest transmuted form, thus freeing and empowering ourselves to be our Divinely Intended Form. Each Human experience is sacred; all of our emotions serve us perfectly. Each time we recognize our human being-ness and choose to love this experience, we are being our Sacred God Goddess Self.

We must not only Claim our Divinity, we must also Recognize our Humanity.

By turning the **8** of heaven above earth to the Infinity (∞) of heaven beside earth, we can fee ourselves of the illusion of separation or the "less/more than's". Think of holding one hand up, receiving the divine plan, and one hand down, loving the human experience we are the alchemist, the magician with the infinity symbol over our heads. Balancing our fear with our Love. The left hand up receiving infinite abundance, and he right hand down sending forth our love and being at peace with our humanness.

Place Hand on Heart and Speak Out Loud:

"I release all judgment and condemnation of humanity, myself, life and of my relationships."

"I invite all my undesired emotions of_ (fill in blank) _____into love, because this part of me has never known love. I thank the angels for doing this for me."

"I invite all disliked, dis-owned, hidden and abandoned parts of me into love. I thank the angels for doing this for me.

"I acknowledge each emotion and thought form I have and love and accept these emotions and thoughts as perfect information that allows me discernment through divine understanding and I now choose to create the Life I am intended."

"I claim my highest, sovereign, free, divinely intended form in the now".

LIGHT ACTIVATION PLAY-SHEET

As Above ~So Below. As With-In So ~With-Out.

Shifting the 8 to the Infinite

∞

I take back my Sacred Power to be a CO-CREATOR BEING! I Honor my Sacred Power.

I Claim my Sacred Value, Worth, Purpose & Being....

My human experience is sacred, My Co-Creations are sacred.

Dark is Sacred, Light is Sacred.

INTO THE LIGHT.....	**CLAIMING MY GOOD.....**
Revealing the dark....	Transcending duality...
Identify ones undesirable emotional experiences with Self-Love and Self-Acceptance.	Identify the Highest Divinely Intended Idea for each situation.
List out the judgments, and negative's experienced.	List and Claim with free will and conscious choice the Divinely Intended Idea.

In the name of the ALPHA & OMEGA, I call forth the Sacred White Fire of Purity to BLAZE, BLAZE, BLAZE, the Light of Ten-Thousand Suns through me and everyone!

52

3. You are not alone!

We are never alone. It is only an illusion of separation when we have felt alone. Unfortunately, if you have felt alone and thought so, then you have inadvertently shut yourself off from your angels and guides. Begin today to invite all of your angels and guides to assist you in standing in your light, and to help you in slaying the demons, obstacles, and freeing you from all human suffering or bondage. If faith or belief is in question, ask your guides to physically demonstrate their presence in your life. It is always our birthright to ask and receive answers or confirmation. Begin to utilize the following tools to assist you in standing in your light: Invocation, Releasing Contracts, Violet Flame Decree's, and Claiming Your daily Victory. The following guides have asked me to share their presence in these guidelines.

Place Hand on Heart and Speak Out Loud:

"I call on all my Angels, Guides and Spirit helpers from the realms of illuminated truth. I thank all my Angels, Guides and Spirit Helpers for assisting me today and every day. Even if I say, I'm alone again."

Spirit Guides, Spirit Helpers and our very own ***"TEAM LIGHT"*** are Ascended Masters, Saints, Guru's, Avatars, God's, Goddesses, Totem Animals, Mythological Creatures and Humans. Spirit demonstrates self and divine guidance through every facet of our lives. Spirit our Higher-Self is ready to assist Humans in becoming Empowered Co-Creators.

The following guides have asked me to share their presence in these guidelines.

Archangel Uriel is the Angel of Light and Divine Order,

he states, *"I am the Light of God"* and asks you to decree this affirmation for yourself as well. Archangel Uriel will assist you every time you decree *"I stand in My Light"* or invoke: *"Light, Light, Light, The Light of God fills me and moves through me. The light of God fills every pore and molecule of my being. Light, Light, Light, I am Light. Light fills my world and all of my relationships".* *"Only Divine Order resides in my mind, Only Divine Order resides in my body. Only Divine Order resides in my Life". "Only Divine Order now resides I every aspect of my life and every relationship and situation I now experience".*

Archangel Michael is the Angel of Divine Purpose, Will, Power, and Protection. He is known as the warrior angel. He is always ready to assist you in overcoming all fear, obstacles, and danger. Archangel Michael supports each who call on him in becoming strong by having the courage to take action for freedom, liberation and safety. Archangel Michael comes to anyone who calls for him. When Michael answers a call he comes with the Angelic 144,000. Legions of Blue Light. Ready to take orders through the Heart of One as self.

It is not the angel who is protecting us. Rather it is the god goddess self as an individualized aspect of god, through the power of the One Heart that is taking back the personal power intended through the law of One Heart to be free, clear and safe.

Through the Power of the One Heart and One Crystalline Christ Consciousness in me.

"I call on Archangel Michael to clear all obstacles, remove all unwanted psychic entities, energies, chords or attachments.

I call on Archangel Michael to now clear all unsafe situations, danger or anything else that keeps me from safety or freedom.

I call on Archangel Michael for Divine Protection of myself and my family.

Cosmic Victory is a Violet Rayed Being. He comes in on mighty wings of cosmic victory. Every time you claim victory, your good, and your success, Mighty Victory will step in to assist you in being successful in all divinely intended purposes. His symbol is the six-pointed star.

"I Claim my Divinely Intended Good today and every day. I Claim my divinely intended Success today and every day. I Claim Victory in this Process!"

Ascended Lady Master the Goddess of Liberty, is excited to make herself known to you today. She has been represented to us in the United States as the Statue of Liberty. Lady Liberty is here to assist all in freeing themselves from all human suffering, pain, and bondage. She states that when you call on her, she will assist you in liberating yourself from any miss-qualified creations. Her torch is the flame of Illumination; she carries the book of Divine Law (order) and the book of Illumination. This knowledge always shows the way out of human error. As you choose to stand in your light, imagine holding up her torch in front of you to light the way, and burn through all obstacles.

"I Stand in my Light. I follow Truth from my Heart. I hold up my Torch. My Torch burns through all obstacles and Lights my Intended Pathway."

REALMS OF DIVINE GUIDANCE

Realms of Divine Guidance are accessible to humans who are open to receive and ask for the Divine Guidance to be revealed to them through their own sacred heart knowing. Most people are already being guided through the hierarchy's of light. Increased conscious awareness and spiritual development improves one understanding of the demonstration of guidance increases through the communal relationships humans have with all sentient beings through multiple dimensions from the past, present and future. Taking time to learn about the Spiritual Hierarchy presented in spiritual religions, philosophies, mystery schools and theosophical texts provides Source with an intelligent channel to put down soul guidance through the language of symbolism, coincidence, metaphor, and synchronicity and through the humans extrasensory intuitive powers.

The following is a list of Individuated Guides experienced and known by many through the inner knowing of the sacred heart and extrasensory perceptions as channels of spiritual guidance. For traditional theosophical and mystery school teachings the councils of guides are called the Spiritual Hierarchy. Third dimensional realities are hierarchical. These are Councils of Light in the Fifth dimensional realities in which humans are fully empowered and choosing to co-create the divine plan in form as heaven on earth. This allows the human to recognize that each of the guides in the spirit realm are the servant, and waiting on the awakened human to give directions and instructions for the hierarchies. The realms of the celestial and elemental are in alliance with humanity. Humans are the engineers of the Plan through conscious intentions. The celestial realm deliver the supplies and the elementals build the structures. Each is an integral part of the co-creation of heaven on earth. Humans are the Gods and Goddess equal to the Ascended Masters and intended to be Ascended Masters in the Now.

In the personal transformational process of ascension, many humans experience comfort through the guidance of the spiritual realm. The Spiritual Realm speaks to humanity through the language of the soul. Many individuals begin to become conscious of spiritual guidance through the extrasensory perceptions of seeing color, hearing messages, feeling of knowing something. One method of increasing Intuitive and Psychic development is to become educated in a body of spiritual wisdom. Such as learning about the Archangels, their colors, frequencies, qualities, virtues and other celestial attributes. As the human begins to ask the higher- self for divine guidance, the higher-self will deliver this guidance through the spiritual wisdom the human has studied and through the humans extrasensory perceptions, dreams, outer realities, animals and every other aspect of everyday living.

The Archangels are easy for many to learn about and integrate into their current cultural wisdom. The angels are mentioned in many world religions and spiritual philosophies. The simplest place to begin, is to learn about the seven archangels and their corresponding colors, musical notes and virtues. These will be returned through the inner knowing when the human asks the higher-self/atman for guidance. Another way it to purchase an oracle card deck and pull a card daily to tune into the energy guidance of the day or question.

COUNCELS OF LIGHT. Octaves of Source Intelligence…..

ONE LIGHT AS A RAINBOW OF DIVINE GUIDENCE: The Transcended Universe. (He who cannot be named) Source Energy described as the Fountainhead.

Ruby Red Ray of the Divine Life Force.

Rose-Orange Ray of Divine Joyful Creative Expression.

Golden Yellow Ray of Divine Illumination, Intelligence and Understanding

Emerald Green Ray of Divine Truth, Science and Healing

Sapphire Blue Ray of Divine Purpose, Will and Devotion

Amethyst Violet Ray of Divine Freedom, Mastery and Transmutation

Sacred White Fire of Purity and Unified Divinity

The seven musical notes. C, D, E, F, G, A, B.

ANGELS OF THE RAYS, The Un-manifest Universe. The unseen spiritual or celestial realm.

Ray 1 The Will of God, Power, Purpose, Protection, and Peace. Known through Crown Chakra

Archangel twins, Michael & Faith. The angel of protection fulfilling Divine Will. He states *"Who is Like God"* or *"I AM my God Goddess Self Today"* He is always ready to assist you in overcoming all fear, obstacles, and danger. Archangel Michael comes to anyone who calls for him. When Michael answers a call he comes with heavens legions of blue light beings, all to keep you safe and free. Michael is there remover of obstacles and energetic chords between souls bound together. He will hand you a blue sward of light to cut through all fear, darkness and obstacles. *"I AM as God Created Me." I AM the Action of God Goddess in human form." "I Claim Freedom and command all energetics attached to me or feeding from, me to release me know. I thank Archangel Michael and his legions of blue light to do this for me".* Michael comes in on the First Ray of God the Sapphire Blue Ray. Michael's twin angel is Faith, faith is needed to fulfill ones divine purpose. Some may know Archangel Michael as the patron saint of firefighters and policemen. He shows himself to me as a large red fire truck.

Ray 2, The Wisdom of God, Love and Understanding. Known through Heart Chakra.

Archangel twins, Jophiel & Christine. "I Am the Beauty of God" "I Claim the Beauty Way" "Divine Order now resides here" "Divine Order & Beauty now reside in everyone, everywhere and everything." Jophiel assists in clarity and revelation of divine purpose and the path way. Jophiel's twin angel is Christine. It is through crystalline consciousness that one expresses the fulfillment of the divinely intended plan in form. Golden, Orange Ray of Illumination.

Ray 3 The Love of God, Creative Expression and Intelligence. Expressed through Throat Chakra.

Archangel twins, Chamuel & Charity. "He who sees God", "I AM the Love of God". "The Love of God resides in me". Chamuel assists in the restoration of unconditional love in relationships and life. In the spirit of joyful Chairty through free-will and choice the soul experiences and fulfills the love that is the intended truth of sacred being. Rose-Pink/Ruby Red Ray of Unconditional Eternal Transfiguring Christ Love.

Ray 4 The Purity of God. Transfiguration and Resurrection. Activated in the Root Chakra.

Archangel twins, Gabriel & Hope. Gabriel is the messenger angel in three world religions. Gabriel may show up in one's life, with the message of activation of the soul's divine purpose. Gabriel assists one is having the strength and courage to live with an open radiant heart of love and light. Archangel Gabriel states, *The Strength of God Resides in me. I AM the Strength of God*". Gabriel comes in the color ray of Aquamarine Blue and White Ray of Purity. Gabriel's twin flame in Hope. Without hope, one does not have strength to live openheartedly empowered as God Goddess in temporary human form. Blue and White Ray of Purity and Divine Protection.

Ray 5 Divine Plan, Science of Divine Order. Known and Expressed through the singular Third Eye Chakra.

Archangel twins, Raphael is the Angel of Healing. Raphael states, "I Am the Healing Power of God." "The Healing Power of God is Activated in me, Resides in me and is Restored in me." Divine Mother Mary is his twin Angel. Mary hold the immaculate concept in place for all newborn souls. It is through the receptive feminine channels that an individual is healed. Emerald Green Ray of Precipitation, Healing and Truth.

Ray 6 Peace of God. Divine Fellowship of Brotherhood & Sisterhood. Radiated with Solar Plexus Chakra.

Archangel twins, Uriel & Aurora. Angel of Light and Divine Order, states, "I am the Light of God" and asks you to decree this affirmation for yourself as well. Archangel Uriel will assist you every time you decree *"I stand in My Light"* or invoke: *"Light, Light, Light, The Light of God fills me and moves through me. The light of Goddess fills every pore and molecule of my being. Light, Light, Light, I am Light. Light fills my world and all of my relationships".* *"Only Divine Order now resides in me, my life and this situation."* Uriel comes in on the Golden Ray or Yellow. Uriel's twin angel is Aurora. Aurora is the light activated with in the dark to illuminate divine truth and heal duality. Gold and Indigo Ray of Peace, Compassion, Devotion, and Celebration.

Cosmic Victory is a Violet Rayed Being. He comes in on mighty wings of cosmic victory. Every time you claim victory, your good, and your success, Mighty Victory will step in to assist you in freeing yourself from all obstacles. His symbol is the six-pointed star. *"I claim my success today and every day, I claim my good today and every day. I claim freedom today and every day. I Claim Victory is this Process!"* Violet and Gold Ray.

Ray 7 Freedom of God, Self-Mastery and Transmutation. Regenerated through the Sacral Chakra.

Archangel twins, Zadkiel & Amethyst. Angels of Alchemy, Eternal Forgiveness, Divine Reconciliation and Transformation. Archangel Zadkiel is the Angel of Divine Mercy. Twin Angel Amethyst magnifies the virtues of forgiveness and regeneration through the crystalline conscious of the violet flame and amethyst crystal. *"I AM the Forgiveness of God." "The Forgiveness of God resides in me and my life."* As co-creator humans do not need to know how. However we must be open to the what. *"I AM open to experiencing Eternal Forgiveness. I thank the Angels for restoration of eternal forgiveness through my entire past, present and future." "All is reconciled through the healing love of God Goddess."* Violet Ray of Transmutation, Freedom, and Liberation.

Ray 8, Liberator of the Fire of Sacred Fire of the Seven Rays.

Archangel Uzziel, Ascension Chamber of the Sacred Heart. Transcends all duality, and illusions of space and time, *"I now Decree through the Unified Power of the One Heart, One Truth and Christ in Me"* Ray of the Sacred White Fire, transcending all duality into Cosmic Consciousness.

DEVIC REALM OF MATTER/ DIVINE MOTHER. The Manifest Universe through the Elements. The realm of matter and physical form.

Divine Mother Earth Beings such as crystals, animals, totems, mythological creatures, plants, minerals and elementals. 7 Rays and 5 Elements.

The directors of element are exponential in the consciousness awareness of the awakened co-creator. As one begins to master being a creator in form they begin to see into the molecular structure of the universe. All the elementals communicate with humans through with fohat/ chi or life source held in matter and known or understood in the unified sacred heart. The elemental beings repeatedly bind source into matter through the reoccurring patterns of sacred geometry known as the platonic solids.

Communing with the inner telluric realms at the micro-level is awakened in the individual open to communing with Mother Nature through the dimensions of matter. This Superpower activated in the Co-Creator allows the being to receive guidance in every aspect of sacred life. It also allows the co-creator to free the elemental being bound to this form through command and permission. Thus transmuting earthly experience of hellish miss-qualified forms. This communion with the elemental real also restores the co-creators ability to experience miraculous healing in self and others.

PLATONIC SOLIDS: Are examples of reoccurring systematic patterns that bind the molecular structure of the universe in matter. These patterns are inherent in all third dimensional forms. The Science of Sacred Geometry is one of the spiritual healing systems within the earth, mineral and crystal world. As follows: Tetrahedron, Fire (4 triangular sides). Hexahedron, Earth (6 square sides). Octahedron, Air, (8 triangular sides). Dodecahedron, Universe of Ether (12 pentagonal sides). Icosahedron, Water (20 triangular sides).

Universe, Ether (12 pentagonal sides). Elohim: Elohim of the Seven Rays: Manifest Universe through the Rays. Twin- flames, Known as the Seven Mighty Elohim in mystery schools. (Elohim of the Ray names are the traditional theosophical names taught in many mystery schools.) Some individuals will be in communion with the Elohim of the Rays and other guides, with other names from different perspectives of the inner sacred heart awareness's. The names of the Elohim from a theosophical approach support the soul process in clearing the elemental bodies of the records of trauma. Through the mythologies of earlier societies and ancient cultures. One example is the myth of "Hercules and the 12 Labors" which is the story of the human god mastering the divine virtues of the solar hierarchy.

Ray 1, Hercules and Amazonia. Divine Plan is manifested through the Strength, Will, Power, Purpose, and Protection of Source as Eternal Peace in the Sacred Heart and Mind of Co-Creator Being. **Be the Ordered Co-Creator of Source.**

Ray 2, Apollo and Lumina. Divine Plan is Revealed and Illuminated through Divine Understanding in the Sacred heart and Mind as the Unified Heart of One-Love. Internal wisdom and external knowledge is understood and unified in the Sacred Heart of Being. **Know and Understand Divine Order**

Ray 3, Heros and Amora. Divine Plan is co-created through the Action of God Goddess as Sound, Vibration, Frequency and Intention through the Unified Sacred Heart and Mind of Co-Creator Being. The genius and intelligence of source is manifest through the aligned action of co-creator. **Create Divine Order through the action of Source in Form.**

Ray 4, Purity and Astrea. Divine Plan is Purified through the caduceus action of the sacred white fire burning through the dross of misaligned energetics bound at the molecular level of being. The raising of the Kundalini. **Purify all to be Divinely Ordered through the Caduceus Action of the Sacred White Fire.**

Ray 5, Cyclopea and Virginia. Divine Plan in action through manifestation of Divine Order and Beauty. Cosmic Sight is restored in Co-Creator as God Goddess seeing through the single eye of Source. **Out of chaos comes order. Imagine, Envision, Invoke and Activate Divine Order in every aspect of life to restore Beauty.**

Ray 6, Peace and Aloha. Divine Plan is restored as Co-Creator Being the Center of Peace. Centered in Eternal Peace extending Love and Well Being through the fellowship of Man. Where each being lifts their fellow man in light, love and praise. **Be Forgiveness, Extend Compassion, Love and Understanding as forgiving Source through the Unified Sacred Heart and Mind of Co-Creator.**

Ray 7, Arcturus and Victoria. Divine Plan is mastered through the alchemical process of Illumination. Unifying illusionary duality through the One Unified Heart as an Eternal Omni-Aware Being in temporary human form. **Divine Order is restored through Love and Acceptance of Team Light and Team Dark as Unified in One-Love.**

Elementals as Directors of the Elements, corresponding to the platonic solids. The five elements through the Solar Hierarchy. (Traditional theosophical names)

AIR, SYLPHS, Aries & Thor, (Twin Flames) Hierarchs of the air element.

Octahedron, Air, (8 triangular sides)

Aires and Thor direct the activities of illumination that proceed from the Mind of Christ. Inspiration, respiration, breathing in and out of the breath of the Holy Spirit, Purification of the air element, atmosphere and the mental belt. Bearers of the prana of the Holy Spirit that is the very life breath of the soul serve with the hierarchies of Aries, Taurus and Gemini to teach mankind the mastery of the mental body. Serve with the hierarchies of Gemini, Libra, and Aquarius to teach the mastery of the air element.

WATER, UNDINES, Neptune & Luara, (Twin Flames) Hierarchs of the water element

Icosahedron, Water (20 triangular sides).

Neptune is the king of the deep. Neptune caries a trident as a symbol of the threefold flame and his authority over the action of the Christ (crystalline) consciousness. Luara is the mother of the tides governing cycles of fertility and the water element as it effects the emotional body. Communications of mankind's emotions, joy, grief, guilt, anger, and love through his astral plan strongly influence the collective unconscious of mankind. Overseers of water and govern tides of the sea and the waters under the sea, precipitation over the land and purification of the water everywhere including in the human body. Live wherever water is found. Sometimes appearing as mermaids. Serve with the hierarchies of cancer, Leo and Virgo to teach mankind mastery of the emotional body. They also teach mastery of the water element in the physical and etheric bodies and the balance of the threefold flame through that element under the hierarchies of Pisces cancer and Scorpio.

EARTH, GNOMES and ELVES, Virgo & Pelleur, Hierarchs of the Earth element

Hexahedron, Earth (6 square sides).

Rule from the sun of even pressure in the middle of the earth and direct the rays of the causal body through the earth element. The binding force at the center of every molecule. Director of the earth element, the mother and father of the Earth Gnome work with the hierarchs of Libra Scorpio and Sagittarius to teach mankind the mastery of the physical bodies and with the hierarchs of Capricorn, Taurus and Virgo to teach them the mastery of the earth element. Tend the cycles of the earth in the four seasons.

The purge the planet of poisons and pollutants that is too dangerous to the plants, humans, and animals. Transmitters of the love of the creator through the beauty and caring of the nature. Wield the fire of the atom and molecule that hold the balance of the continents and form

FIRE, SALAMANDERS, Oromasis and Diana Hierarch of the fire element

Tetrahedron, Fire (4 triangular sides).

Serve with hierarchies of Capricorn Aquarius and Pisces to teach mankind the mastery of the etheric plane and with Aries Leo and Sagittarius in teaching the mastery of the fire element. Work closely with the etheric or fire body of man in mastering the caduceus action and in opening the seven charkas in addition to regulating the flow of light through the charkas and in aligning the four lower bodies. Quick and intensify the action of the fire in the threefold flame and any call of mankind, i.e. prayer.

ONLY LOVE IS REAL!

The Octaves of Light, have been known by many as the Spiritual Hierarchy. In truth, Humans who have Sacred Dominion as Free-Will are the beings who are freeing the Spiritual Hierarchy, and collective consciousness of Mother Earth. It is not necessary to be in communion with spirit guides to ascend. However the language of spirit as symbolism, metaphor, angels, totems, color, vibration, frequency. Geometry and more, is easily understood through the natural intuitive process of divine guidance.

Each body of wisdom the human chooses to become familiar with allows the Higher-Self to guide the human through returning of this wisdom through the inner intuitive awareness of divine knowing through the Sacred Heart.

I AM THE LIGHT, I AM THE TRUTH, I AM THE WAY

I AM THE TRUTH.

"I See Divine Truth", "I am the Sight of God", "I See as God Sees"

1. **Be open to seeing the Divinely Intended Plan.**

How would God, Buddha, Jesus, or Gandhi see this situation? When most people act badly, they are doing so from their own place of pain or suffering. People, who are in pain, need more love not less. As you open yourself up to seeing as God sees, it is easy to become aware of this.

The green ray is the ray of truth, order, science and spirituality. It is the ray of the Goddess (showing herself as Queen of Heaven) and Archangel Raphael, the angel of healing. As you imagine the green ray of truth and divine order fanning out in front of you, from your third eye, it puts the path of illuminated truth in front of you. When we claim our birthright to see truth it lifts all in our lives up into the blue ray of the divine blueprint. When we see this divinely intended plan, we can then begin to declare it as already happening. This is where we take back our power to be co-creator beings, creating Heaven on Earth.

Now declare that only Love, and only Divine Order now works through any situation that is less than the divinely intended idea. If the situation seems unjust, Declare that Divine Justice now works in this situation. Lady Portia is the Goddess of Justice, (Portia comes in on the violet ray of freedom) she will act on your behalf to assure God's Divine Justice now happens.

> **Place Hand on Heart and Speak Out Loud:** *"I Claim my Cosmic Sight. I claim the Beauty Way, I now see the Divine Order and Divine Beauty that is the Divine Plan, in everyone, everywhere and everything."*

66

2. Choose for the 'Highest Good"

Choosing to know what is for your own and others highest good does not mean to push away the human experience of suffering. Rather we must balance the polarities of "Seeing as God Sees", and feeling as we currently do. Both can happen at once. It is important to anchor your higher-self within your heart to assist in this process. This is the part of you that is one with God. Previously it has been above our head, and now we will pull it down through a cord of light and anchor it in our heart. "My higher-self now resides in me; Divine Understanding is now activated in me. I now open myself to know higher truth through my own understanding." All choices I now make are for my highest good.

> *Place Hand on Heart and Speak Out Loud: "I Choose for my Divine Good as intended in the Divine Plan in every experience with ease."*

3. Your Being Always Knows Truth

Place your hand on your heart every time you might need an answer to any question regarding truth. The heart is the physical location that connects with both your higher spiritual self and your human self. It is through the sacred flame in our heart that we have the divine birthright to know all we wish to know. The KEY IS TO ASK! It may take a few days or hours for the answer to be revealed to you. All you need to do is ask and be open to receive the answer. Spirit responds through synchronicity, symbols, and coincidences. Anything brought to your attention three or more times is an answer.

SACRED HEART ON BOARD GUIDENCE SYSTEM.
Body Pendulum: Practice this Exercise....

> Learn about the body pendulum and begin to practice muscle testing to discern it for yourself. Place your hand on your heart and ask your body to show you YES. Do not lock your knees; your body will naturally sway towards one direction, usually towards the front. Now ask your body to show you NO, usually you will

sway to the rear. Now ask your body a question such as "my name is_____". Let your body answer through the sway. If your sway does not move forward and back, then learn to balance your chakras and it will begin to do so. You can also utilize muscle testing, or any other form of kinesiology to discern truth. Try it, it works!

I am the light, I am the truth, I am the way.

I AM THE WAY

1. **I Open Myself to Be the Way. Place hand on Sacred Heart and Speak Out-Loud through the Power of the Spoken Word.**

   "I open myself to know the Way", "I open myself to have the Way", and "I open myself to be the Way", "I Am the Way"

This is your divine creative power, the power to create heaven on Earth. Humans have free will. We can begin to monitor our thoughts 24 hours a day, 7 days a week. All of our thoughts go out before us and begin to manifest in physical form what they are. Thought patterns that we have had for years or lifetimes have momentum. They are like big rolling wheels. When we stop having these thoughts, the wheel does not stop moving immediately. We must begin to build another momentum of new thought patterns. In a lower vibrational world it takes about THREE MONTHS for a new thought pattern that is given energy every day, to begin to roll on its own without feeding it. CHOOSE to hold thoughts of love, thoughts of divine order, in all ways. CHOOSE to have compassion and love for your own suffering, and miss-creations. CHOOSE to forgive yourself every day and in every way. CHOOSE to forgive others every day and each time they repeat the same bad behavior, remember they are coming from a place of pain. You do not have to know how to forgive; you must only be open to forgiving for forgiveness to happen.

2. Self-First!

Yes, this is right, self-first. You are a Divine Light Being, a God Goddess of Earth. There is no separation between self and spirit. Everything you do for yourself you do for all that is. If you deny yourself on the basis of "selfishness is bad", then you deny all that is. Each time you have denied what is in your heart, you have sacrificed yourself and all of angelic humanity with this. Over time this self-sacrifice manifests as the experience or others sacrificing and betraying us. When we say no to our Sacred Heart, others and our higher-self, say no to us. When we say yes to our Sacred Heart, God, our higher-self and others say yes to us. Now is the time to not only claim your divinity, but to also acknowledge your hearts deepest desires. For what is in your own heart is also within the Heart of Humanity. In the past we have used our mind, our intellect and rational thinking to hide, ignore and keep hidden what is in our hearts. We have told ourselves that emotions are bad and weak. These same emotions bring us our greatest joy, bliss, and happiness. NOW IS THE TIME TO HONOR YOUR HEART! The sacred space which holds our divinity, our truth, our light and the Way! As you open yourself to know what your deepest hearts desires are hold them up in front of you and begin to use your intellect and rational thinking to obtain them, you are creating Heaven on Earth. Become the action of God. *"I Am the Action of God"*. Become the passion of God, *"I Am the Passion of God"*, after all, as a God, I would only create Humanity to have fun.

3. Rescind and Release all Contracts of Obligation and Responsibility.

Place hand on Sacred Heart and Speak Out-Loud through the Power of the Spoken Word.

"I now release any and all soul level contracts or agreements that I have ever made in any lifetime that I am obligated to or responsible for; the mother, father, husband, wife, brother, sister, children, friends, church, community, humanity, employer, co-workers, neighborhood, anyone, anywhere at any time. I am now free to create new realities. I claim my birthright to be free and create new realities. I now choose to create that it is always safe for me to take

care of me first. I now only draw towards me people, situations, and events that honor this, and where it is always safe for me to take care of me first. The more I open to receive, the more abundant and at peace I will be. If I choose to care for others it is now from my desire, my love and because it brings me joy, not through obligation. As I honor myself, others honor me."

I AM my Christ Self Today. I AM THE LIGHT, THE TRUTH and THE WAY.

I AM the Light, I Stand in My Light, Light, Light, Light, I AM Light, All is revealed in Light.

I AM the Truth, I know the Truth, I have the Truth, I Stand in My Truth!

I AM the Way, I know the way, I have the way, and I AM the Way!

I Choose to Co-Create Heaven on Earth Today.

ONLY LOVE IS REAL!

Beginning Routines for the Path of Enlightenment, The process of Becoming Light!

Continuous Daily Self-Care Routines and practices are picked up by the sub-conscious self and carried forward into our waking life.

The Seventh Ray is the ray of mastery, transmutation, ceremony, magic and ritual. It is through "Continuous Daily Self-Care Routines" that the individual gains self-mastery. A practice of constant daily routines or rituals build a strong energetic foundation for anchoring of the Solar Light Body.

1. **Being Heart Centered:** The Heart Chakra is our Divine Center. An Open Radiant Heart is a Crystalline Heart. It allows us to access all unconscious, past, future, and current wisdom we would

like to know. This wisdom is revealed to our inner knowing by asking with intent. The Heart is where the multidimensional being unifies into the one unified truth. A simple way to be heart centered is to place your hand on your heart, while requesting information, setting intention or sending healing.

2. **Live in the Now with Conscious Deliberate Intent.** Set intent to be mindful, present & centered. Choose to Live in the Now. Allow oneself to be filled with Higher-self, the Embodiment of Spirit. Live from the Heart. Practice using the mind to obtain what is in the heart not hide what is in the heart. The heart is not rational, the mind is… Choose people, places and situations that raise the body's vibrational frequencies. Always choose from the sacred heart for the highest good of the unified self.

3. **Grounding the body to Galactic Heart of the central Sun and to the Global Heart of Mother Earth with Guided Imagery**: Imagine or envision one's body with roots to the center of Earth from the base of the spine & soles of the feet and from the crown of one's head to the center of the central sun. Sometimes it is helpful to imagine oneself as a tree in this exercise. Each individual's energetic space is from the center of mother earth to the center of the great central sun. This is our whole column of light as an Eternal Being.

   a. ENERGY FLOWS: Two continuous spiraling flows of energy the Ida and Pingala, flow from the center of the earth up through the spine, the central channel called the sutruma, to the center of the central sun and from the center of the central sun down through the spine to the center of the earth. This may be visualized as DNA Spirals. These energy channels flow through each chakra center until we evolve into our Radiant Solar Light Body Selves. Each chakra receives the energy required for balance. Blockages in energy flow may cause chakras energy vortexes to spin irregularly leading to either deficient, or excessive energies in these centers. It is helpful to ground any wound or injury to both the earth and sun.

Also one can ground a home, room, vehicle or anything. This creates a radiant empowering protective matrix, our light-body supporting the ascension process. Learning and practicing the Star Merkaba Mediation and Building the Rainbow Bridge is recommended in this process,

4. **Muscle Testing: Trusting Self and Divine Guidance. SACRED HEART ON BOARD GUIDENCE SYSTEM. Body Pendulum:** Learn about the body pendulum and begin to practice muscle testing to discern it for yourself. Place your hand on your heart and ask your body to show you YES. Do not lock your knees; your body will naturally sway towards one direction, usually towards the front. Now ask your body to show you NO, usually you will sway to the rear. Now ask your body a question such as "my name is_____". Let your body answer through the sway. If your sway does not move forward and back, then learn to balance your chakras and it will begin to do so. You can also utilize muscle testing, or any other form of kinesiology to discern truth. Try it, it works!

5. **Clearing the Chakra's of others energies.** CLEAR Everyday send all other energy home from your field and bring all you own energy home to your field. Drop the Divine Mind down through the Sacred Heart; look through this mind's eye into each chakra. Visualize each chakra and ask if anyone or thing is attached there. Through the Power of Divine Revelation, Ask it to reveal itself. Ask how many other energies or people (that are not your own), are connected to this chakra, ask each to be clearly revealed. Ask each to show itself to you and what qualities it is connected too. This will help you to understand any karmic ties that may be binding one. Now send each one back to its sender or the center of Mother Earth. Command one's own energy to be returned to self. Repeat this process until clear. Scan the rest of the body, with the same process. Next, imagine the aura as a Bubble of Light around the body, radiating brilliant fiery light. Seal any holes or tears in the

aura, commanding any attachments to clear. Ground the aura light body to earth and sun.

> **Place Hand on Heart and Speak Out Loud:** *Until clear, ask daily, How many other peoples are energetically attached to me? I ask them to be revealed to me. What body part or chakra are they attached too? The location or chakra will give one the information about why this person's energy is chording or attached to oneself. There is always a doorway or energetic agreement that is the opening allowing the other person to chord or attach to us energetically Acknowledge this persons energy and I now Command it to be returned back to this person or Mother Earth to be recycled. I now Command all my own energy to be returned to me. Next time I connect I ask it be through my Sacred Heart Chakra. I ask Higher-Self, the Angels and Elementals to do this for me.*

6. **Balancing Chakras with Intention:** Begin with the root chakra. Visualize the root chakra rooting into the earth; use the hand to clockwise spin this chakra slowly with the intent of balancing. While the hand is spinning the chakra, it is both from the front and back of the vessel. Move next to the sacral chakra, place hand over chakra and spin gently clockwise with intent for balance, continue this process for each chakra When the crown chakra is reached move hand a above head visualizing connection with higher self. Imagine bubble or Ovid of Light around the body and aura about 3 feet big. Imagine placing mirrors in the Ovid/aura facing outwards repelling unwanted frequencies.

Balance the chakras with affirmations, Toning, Mantra and Sound.

As one places hand over each chakra and spins clockwise, affirm a corresponding affirmation out loud. The following are examples. Please feel free to create your own affirmations and to experiment with toning for each chakra the same way.

Root Chakra. *I am Safe, It is Safe to be in my Body. I Belong, I am Grounded. I am connected.*

Sacral Chakra. *I move freely, I am free to move. I am free to express my sacred sexuality safely. I am safe to create. I create freely. I am free to give birth to new forms with ease. I Claim Sacred Pleasure as my Divine Right. It is safe to have and experience pleasure.*

Solar Plexus. *I am safe to have my personal power. My desires are aligned with my Divine Good. I am joyful. I am safe to laugh joyfully. (The full belly laugh)*

Heart Chakra. *I am safe to love. Loving is Safe. It is safe to be heart centered. It is safe to have an open heart. I am heart centered. My heart is a fiery vortex of love. I trust myself. I am open to trusting Divine Guidance from my Sacred Heart.*

Throat Chakra. *I take back my right to express my truth with ease. It is safe to speak my truth. I voice my truth with ease. I am at peace with my truth.*

Third Eye Chakra. *I claim my Divine Sight. It is safe to see truth and guidance. I see beauty and order in my life and my world. My Divine Pathway is revealed to me easily and known by me easily.*

Crown Chakra. *I am connected to Source with ease. I am source energy. I am Light. I claim my cosmic connections, my cosmic knowing, my cosmic being and my cosmic heritage.*

One may balance the Chakras with Sound through toning the following key notes, vowel sounds or traditional Biji Mantras for each chakra through conscious intent. Color may also balance ones chakras.

Chakra	Color	Note/Tone	Vowel Sound	Mantra (Bija) chakra seed syllable
Root	Red	C	UH	Lam
Sacral	Orange	D	OOO	Vam
Solar Plexus	Yellow	E	OH	Ram
Heart	Green	F	AH	Yam
Throat	Blue	G	I	Ham
Third Eye	Indigo	A	AYE	Aum/ Om
Crown	Violet	E	AH	Ahh/Aum

EXERCISE/MEDITATION: Divine Revelation to develop balanced Chakras.

Place Hand on Heart and Speak Out Loud: I ask my Higher Self to reveal to me what animal, color, symbol, crystal, flower or something else, that may support oneself in becoming, enlightened, effective, the highest intended or free for each chakra. One at a time, writing each answer down and researching what this divine guidance is. Remember the answer is delivered in the language of the soul. For those who find it difficult to see with the inner eye, this ability will increase and develop as one becomes open to the experience and claims it.

Another way to do this exercise is to pick a deck or oracle cards, such as an animal medicine deck, and pull one card for each chakra with intent. Meditate on each card and ask the higher-self to integrate and balance each chakra as one does this.

7. **Clearing: A Daily Practice of Divine Detachment.** Every day it is important to send all other peoples energy home. It is natural for our energy bodies and chakra vortex's to energetically connect,

attach, and interact with others. Thoughts and feelings are psychic energy that radiate out and may be directed towards others or band in collective pools that are called entities. These entities may attach to an unknowing host who has a similar resonance. We often draw strength and energy from each other. These connections may stay in place for years unless an individual takes responsibility for his energy and chooses to be clear. Having contacts of Obligation or feeling responsible for another creates a doorway that allows these energies to attach becoming draining. Obligation also sets one up to be responsible for, clear and work through their energy. This piles more energetic weight clouding clarity and the Divinely Intended Freedom.

> **Place Hand on Heart and Speak Out Loud:** *"I Claim Divine Detachment as my Birthright. I now Love ALL people and all people Love me Without Attachment!"*

> *"I am the only thinker in my mind and the only feeler in my body."*

> *"I Claim Freedom, Sovereignty and Truth as my Divine Birthright."*

> *"I Claim DIVINE DETATCHMENT as my Inherent Birth Right!*

> *"I Command all other beings energies that are attached to me, feeding from me, draining me, chording me, inhibiting me or binding me, to FREE and RELEASE me now. You are no longer allowed to attach to any part of me. I send everyone else's energy home to them. I call back to me my own energy. I thank the angels and my Higher-Self for doing this for me in the Now.*

> *"From this Day Forward: I Claim Divine Detachment as my Inherent Right. I Now Love all people and all people Love me, without attachment."*

8. **Choose Pleasure for Being:** Become aware of current human choices or behaviors one uses to ground or be in the physical vessel. Yoga, exercise, or foods are some examples. Begin to replace negative habits that ground one-self with positive habits. Some individuals may only experience being in the body through pain. Now is the time to choose pleasure in the body verses pain. It is our purpose to create heaven on earth in and through our human body, not leave the body to go to heaven.

9. **Choose High Vibrating Relationships and Experiences.** Give self-permission to choose life relationships and circumstances that make one feel good and lift one up. These will raise ones vibrational frequencies. Choose daily self-care routines that increase vibrational frequency of being such as coating the body with essential oils, singing, drumming, or listening to positive music. As one detaches from low vibrating relationships it frees the self and other person of the karmic patterns and charges. This allow the other person to also grow and increase frequencies. Sometimes they will come back in a higher form. Other times new individuals that match the current vibration frequency will appear. Like minded, or like attracts like. This is the lesson of Mastery over Outer Conditions.

10. **More Love not Less: Only Love is Real.** All else is an illusion. Each experience is an opportunity to choose again. Each experience is an opportunity to love the self and others through conscious choice, compassion, understanding, and forgiveness. As a multi-dimensional being this may involve setting healthy boundaries, like saying NO in the Physical Realm, while holding the Divine Idea or Immaculate Concept in place, in the Mental Realm. The Emotional Realm may need acknowledgement by inviting the low vibrating emotions into love. As the individual gains self-mastery it becomes easier to integrate the multidimensional experiences through the unified one heart.

CHAPTER 3

---⊙---

Sacred Science of Manifestation

SACRED SCIENCE OF MANIFESTATION, Conscious Co-Creation Formula's...

MANIFESTING, Just for Being

The Science of the Spoken Word is referred to in mystery schools as the science of precipitation. It is a bringing down from the higher mental knowing or guidance into a denser physical experience.

The Higher- Self, Source as Divine Intelligence, presses on the person an idea or aha. This idea may be experienced by the individual as incite or fleeting thought held in the mind or crown and third eye chakra. As the individual acknowledges the idea she can give it voice or write it down, bringing the idea into sound or form on paper through the throat and heart chakra. Next the individual senses how it would feel to experience the idea from the heart chakra and may add to it the action of the second chakra. If the idea is aligned with the greatest good and the individual is unencumbered from outdated energetics, the idea will manifest into physical form, from the dimension of the first chakra.

Every thought form you have moves into the collective consciousness of mankind. This is the astral realm. This thought form then **precipitates,** (like rain) down to earth and becomes what it is in physical form. This process is called **"the Science of the Spoken Word"**.

Think of manifesting as the Down-Flow of energy from Source, through Divine Intelligence. From the spiritual non-tangible world to the physical tangible world. Each human chakra might be through of as a clearing/ awareness station for source energy to manifest in form through the empowered human. The human vessel is like a radio dial. Each chakra is like a channel giving the human information by tuning into a different awareness, frequency or dimension.

The balanced mastery of the original 7 ray lessons or 7 tones corresponding to the chakras of the third dimensional world is Diamond Consciousness. As the Human gains expanded awareness they are able to create a spiraling Column of Light that unifies the Human Heart with the Galactic Heart and Earth Heart. Becoming the Rainbow Bridge of Light. This column of light has been referred to as the Antakarana.

The Sacred Heart electromagnetic field expands exponentially as a Golden Sun. (son of god/logos as divine mind) activating the Solar Light Body and Magical Life, as an unlimited co-creator being with 13 Strands of DNA activated, transcending duality and stepping off the wheel of karma. INSTANT MANIFESTATION, WITH EASE JUST FOR BEING!

Thirteen Dimensions as Heaven on Earth, unified through Cosmic Consciousness is a Paradigm Shift. Referred to as The Golden Age of Enlightenment.

BRIDGE OF LIGHT. Higher Cosmic Consciousness, Higher chakras above our crown. Light spirals through the 8th Dimension, Soul-Star Chakra above the crown infinitely down and upwards as Divine Intelligence, Source Energy, through the unified Heart. Celestial Angelic Realm. **Omni-Awareness as breath of ONE-LOVE.**

1. Crown: Human has an idea or "aha" thought. This is Divine Intelligence of Spirit Higher-Self activating, or putting down a higher guidance. **Knowing the Divinely Intended Plan.**

2. Third Eye: Human acknowledges Divine Intelligence through, cognitions, perceptions, imagery, visualization, and imagining. **Seeing the Divinely Intended Plan.**

3. Throat: Human expresses Divine Intelligence through, Setting Intent, verbalization, writing it down, affirming, invoking, claiming and decreeing. Sound creates form. **Speaking and Activating the Divinely Intended Plan through Sound, Word and Vibration.**

4. Sacred Heart: Human experiences Joy of Divine Intelligence through Divine Understanding and merging mind with heart in the Now. Experiencing life "As If" the sacred intent of Divine Intelligence is already manifested. Transcending Duality by Activating the Sacred-Heart Toroidal magnetic field. Sometimes referred to as the Star- Mer-kaba, Solar-Light Body or Rainbow Bridge. The Power of Unified Love and Understanding. **Understanding the Divinely Intended Plan though Balanced Three Fold Nature of Being.**

5. Solar Plexus: Consciously chosen positive thoughts and positive emotions transcend duality and manifest sacred desire in form. Imprinting the world with through sustained joy, peace and steady focus of feeling the sacred intent as happening now. **Feeling the Divinely Intended Plan as Safe, Peaceful and Empowered.**

6. Sacral: Creative expression of the Sacred Intent, through art, movement, vibration, play and laughter. **Expressing the Divinely Intended Plan through Creative Expression, Vibration and Movement.**

7. Root: Manifestation of Divine Intelligence through Sacred Intent of Sacred Heart into the experience of physical form. The Physical Tangible Demonstration of answers from each question asked of soul/higher-self. **Having the Divinely Intended Plan in Experience and Form.**

BRIDGE OF LIGHT. Inner-Dimensional Consciousness, through the 8th Dimension, Earth-Star Chakra's below the feet and spiraling downward to the Diamond Core Center of One Unified Earth-Heart. Crystalline Consciousness as ONE. The crystalline grid and ley lines of Mother Earth. Devic, Elemental Telluric Realm. The 13th dimension of Magical Elemental Being. **Anchoring the Divine Plan as a transducer, mid-wife or co-creator being LOVE IN CRYSTALLINE CONSCIOUSNESS.**

The Causal Bodies are the layers of energetic dimensions surrounding the human vessel that step down Source-Energy into form or density. Each dimension contains within it all the lower dimensions or causal bodies. The chakras can be thought of as the doorway into each causal body, spectrum or dimension. The chakras supply human vessel source energy "Fohat" through the etheric glandular system corresponding to each chakra. These doorways may also become openings, allowing psychic attachments, chords and entities to control, manipulate, and feed from the human bound to lower states of consciousness. Draining and depleting ones intended infinite supply of source energy. Leading to the illusionary experience of polarization. One may think of these as karmic wheels, where the soul continues to experience both sides of a karmic lesson in self and outer world, until conscious awareness, free-will and choice allow the human to transcend the karmic experience through the Unified Heart. Thus "Stepping off the wheel of karma". When humans AWAKEN with 13 strands of DNA activated, they become free and empowered as co-creators of the Divine Plan.

Once the Heart's magnetic field is activated through the activation of the Solar-Light-Body, Star- Merkaba, or Toroidal Flow the human is able to transcend limitation and take up their rightful place as an Unlimited Being in Temporary Human Form. Some may refer to this as Immortality.

The Human transcends duality through merging the three fold nature in the sacred heart. As a free sovereign being with crystalline consciousness of one, humans are able to align and free the lower causal bodies of the dross energetics that bind one to limitation. The lower causal bodies are the elemental bodies of matter storing the records of karma. Freeing the lower bodies frees the elementals by restoring the sacred white fire center of purity in each molecule. This is restoration of the intended life-source, chi, prana or electrical torus field called Fohat. The Spiritualization of Matter.

In other words, through the Unified Heart of One as Individualized crystalline consciousness of transcended Cosmic Awareness, the empowered human is able to unify the soul's records from this life, past- lives, and non- human lifetimes both on and off planet. Healing all Inter-Species Conflicts The experience of Eternal Peace in Earthly life. This in turn frees the Individual and Elemental Realm of miss-qualified forms, such as suffering, illness, lack and slavery. Manifestation becomes immediate and easy when aligned through the one unified heart as a fiery vortex of one-love.

In the "AHA" moment "precipitation as manifestation" is awareness of the divinely intended plan. Divine Intelligence, happens as the Divine Mind or Logos, meaning consciousness, and is then stepped down through the 7 causal bodies of humans. The same divine order is true of the universe, solar system, Mother Earth and all sentient beings. As Above, So Below. As With-In, So With-Out. The macrocosm is a reflection of the microcosm. Meaning everything a human experiences in their outer-world is also a reflection of soul's records within the DNA or Akashi of the human's inner world. Therefore by clearing the inner-world of sub-conscious and unconscious records, agreements, contracts, or bound relationships, one frees the individualized self. Restoring Unlimited Potential in Human Form. Also meaning that the human who consciously chooses to "Imprint" their Sacred heart Toroidal Field with Sacred Intent through continuous conscious choice, meditation, sound, frequency and repetition will magically manifest these into sacred form with ease. As the Sacred Heart toroidal is a powerful electromagnetic vortex the Ascension Chamber of One. When more than one human being comes together in unified group intent the manifestation of the Golden Age is exponential.

Every *thought* a human has creates a form in the individual's *mental causal body*. Every *word* a human speaks creates a form in the individual's *astral causal body*. The astral causal body is more dense and closer to physical form. This is why speaking the sacred intention out-loud through the POWER OF the SPOKEN WORD as an empowered Being (God Goddess) may manifest the sacred intention into form more quickly than just thinking or writing it. In the Precipitation or manifestation of Sacred Intentions into form, THE SPOKEN WORD is the SUPER-POWER of the Self-Actualized or Divinely Empowered Human. Vibration, Frequency and Sound Create Form.

The Collective Consciousness of human-kind is the sum total of all thoughts, emotions or experiences held by humans. All thoughts are vibration and create an energetic form in the Astral Causal Body of the individual. Over time repetitive thought forms of an individual or family generational patterns band together in the collective causal body of humanity and Mother Earth. Thought forms or emotions that happen repetitively by an individual and through family generations gain momentum and life-force of their own. These are most often identified as entities separate from the individual personal experience. (Referred to as un-transmuted karma, the Guardian at the Gate or Dweller on the Threshold)

In the Third Dimensional World, of duality, of fear based consciousness, it takes up to three months of repeated thought forms to give birth to a new momentum. Old outdated thought forms, (energetics) have momentum. Think of these as a big wheel or ball rolling down a hill. When one stops feeding it with fear based thoughts and emotions, it takes time for the momentum to come to a stop. New thought forms or affirmations spoken repetitively three minutes a day for three months give birth to new momentums that will continue to roll even when we don't think about them for a day. Another formula is to affirm continuously the new empowered thought forms for 21 days in a row. These sacred intentions will become automatic, gain momentum and continue forward momentum in the co- creation of heaven on earth.

Everything in life is impersonal. When life is personal is karmic, meaning charged. Charged energies are karmic and take longer to clear or manifest the new in physical form. Loved joyful desires or experiences without attachment are more immediate to manifest in form.

Each person's causal bodies are like magnets attracting towards them the resonant collective consciousness of other's causal creations. Meaning like attracts like. When these energetic forms gain enough momentum through repetition they become energetics called entities. These entities were created in the absence of love. They were created in the energy of fear, and low vibration as miss-qualified forms. Entities are fearful of losing their life-force energy. An entities life-force is the humans fear and unconscious denied emotions or repetitive negative thoughts and patterns of limitation. If the human acknowledged the emotional experience and limiting thoughts or patterns then invites them into the love, Higher-Self steps in to transform the energy and a different or more desired physical or outer experience will manifest. Our dark emotions such as anger are not less than love. They are just less desired than love. Anger or other dark emotions and thought forms serve humans perfectly providing each soul with a lesson or service, such as motivation, or protection. Humans have free will. Claiming this freedom and choosing alternative experiences is possible and the awakened creator-beings true purpose. It is possible to choose love in every experience.

For the Empowered Human to transmute and free an energetic it is important not to push it away or judge it, as this will feed the low vibration by expanding it in the sub-conscious self. Judgment creates judgement which is a karmic curse. Rather one must acknowledge and thank the energy for doing its perfect work for self, or the evolutionary soul lesson of self and humanity. From a place of dominion centered in the Sacred-Heart one can clear with the violet fire and invite the energetic into the unified heart of one. Allowing this energetic or captivated elemental to be free and shift form and shape into the new supportive structures of unlimited supply.

This is an alchemical process of inviting each rejected or denied experience and emotion into love, through the wisdom flame of the sacred heart or Higher Self. As a human you are not healing clearing or doing this work, rather **you are Sacred Being with Dominion, asking, commanding, inviting, and invoking Higher-Self, or the angels to do this for you.** Humans Free the Elemental Beings from holding, miss-qualified, low vibration forms in place and facilitate or mid-wife the process of freedom through Sacred Dominion as an Empowered Co-Creator of Heaven on Earth.

Transmutation, is the alchemical process of moving from dense experiences to enlightened experiences. Turning lead into gold. Meaning the process of clearing all karmic or hardened energies of separation, limitation and lack that the soul is bound too. As one unifies all experiences through the Unified Heart of One-Love transmutation happens. The Violet Flame is the Sacred Fire of Transmutation. The violet fire is the "scrubby brush" that purifies and clears the individual and collective records of miss-qualified elemental forms. The Violet Flame is the equal balance of the blue flame of power and the pink flame of love in the sacred heart. Divine Equanimity. The Violet Ray is also the Seventh Ray of Freedom, Mastery, Transmutation, and Ritual, meaning daily self-care routines of enlightenment. The Golden Ray is the Wisdom Flame of the Sacred Heart and the place of Divine Understanding as an Unlimited Being. The Violet Flame transmutes the soul records, restoring the Golden Ray of Wisdom as Divine Mind/ Buddha Consciousness is unified with Divine Heart/ Christ Consciousness. The Age of Golden Enlightenment.

When the humans Sacred-Heart Toroidal Field is activated and spinning through awakened higher states of consciousness, Humans will find themselves living in the Fifth Dimensional World. Heart-Math Institute has shown that "The energetic field of the sacred heart is 100,000 times stronger electrically and up to 5,000 times stronger magnetically than the human brain". The Fifth Dimensional World is the Galactic Experience of The Divine Plan Fulfilled for the Universal Brotherhood and Sisterhood of ONE-LOVE.

The Unified Field of intended empowerment is experienced as Consciousness of Infinite Supply, where everything in the world empowers and lifts one up. Instant Manifestation now happens with ease. This is how the implementation of the Divine Plan of Heaven on Earth is happening. As one sets intent from the sacred heart aligned with Divine Mind one can watch it spring forth in form right before one's eyes. The Sacred Heart,

Electrical Activation imprints the world more than the world imprints the human.

For Humans, DIVINE INTELLIGENCE, is simply called cognition. *"Cognition is the process by which the sensory input is transformed, reduced, elaborated, stored, recovered, and used. Cognition is a faculty for the processing of information, applying knowledge, and changing preferences. Cognition, or cognitive processes, can be natural or artificial, conscious or unconscious."* Wikipedia.

As humans we are Multi-Dimensional Beings experiencing multiple experiences at one time. The more heart centered we become the easier it is to detach from the lower vibrations of the third dimensional world of duality and suffering. Through the free-will process of becoming Light, vibrating at a higher frequency of crystalline consciousness of Unconditional Love, we begin to experience our unlimited potential in human form. Through our free-will we have the choice to tell our mind what to think and our body what to feel daily. As we shift our cognitions through the awareness of Individualized Choice, Free-Will, Unconditional Love, and Conscious Deliberate Intent we become free to experience Abundance and Peace throughout every facet of our lives as Heaven on Earth.

Humans have a conscious, sub-conscious and unconscious mind.

The subconscious mind does not know the difference between third dimensional reality and imagined reality. Whatever thought, envisioned, imagined, heard or spoken repeatedly is picked up by the sub-conscious mind and projected into our reality. Without this awareness the subconscious mind can become chaotic, thus creating a chaotic life experience. It is important to make a commitment to practice living with conscious deliberate intent every moment.

By being two people at once one can transcend the dual experiences and effectively create the new matrix, reality or paradigm. The first person as self, is experiencing the reality with self-love, forgiveness and compassion for the sacred human experience, even if it is painful. The second person as self, is choosing the new reality as intended through divine understanding and activating the divine plan in each moment through intent, sound, frequency and vibration.

Super Conscious Mind: Higher-Self as Divine Mind. Sometimes referred to as the Atman. The part of soul- self that is unified with source at all times. The Atman does not engage with the everyday human until the human engages with the Atman, Higher-self. Usually this is through prayer, journaling, affirmation, invocation, dreams, intuition and meditation. Then the Higher-Self Atman will "put-down" answers, information, guidance and divine understanding from with-in the Sacred Heart Knowing. **The process of Human Invocation is responded to by Spirit/ Source as Evocation. This formula is how one builds a unified column of light as the "Rainbow Bridge or Antakarana".** The Higher-Self may be directed through the Sacred-Heart to go out ahead in "perceived time" to remove obstacles and provide for multi-dimensional needs in and out of form. All causal bodies or multi-dimensional aspects of self are aligned through the Solar Logos of Divine Intelligence, as Super-Conscious Mind.

Conscious Mind: The conscious self is the known information or cognitions one is aware of in the Now. The conscious mind is experienced through our reality as time, and space in the third dimension. **Experienced as the reasoning mind, ego and director of the personality.** Self-governing structures including the ways, means and measure of how one organizes self and life. The rational mind or ego is often placed in the driver seat until the Higher-Self is invited to be the driver of self. The conscious mind is the Free-Will Executive of personal power of will-power. To choose is to will. Choices aligned with higher-self are creating the Divine a Plan in form and are expansive for the soul's evolution. Choices not aligned with Divine Good, bind the soul to karma, limitation, illness and slavery. Mammalian Brain.

Sub-Conscious Mind: The sub-conscious self is known, yet not what one is consciously aware of in the now. Such as being asked to remember an event at a childhood birthday party. It examines, classifies and stores information. **The sub-conscious non-reasoning mind is the memory bank of thoughts, feelings, imagination, habitual patterns impulses,**

trauma and desires. It controls the physical body as operator of the automatic nervous system. Regulator of relaxation or anxiety. Works 24/7. Creates dreams and vital life-source energy. Controls inner senses such as visualization and imagination. Creates threads of energy that contact both objects and people. Does not know the difference between experienced life and reality in the third dimensional world and the dream or imaginary world. Is animalistic instinctual and territorial. Reptilian Brain.

Un-Conscious Mind: the Unconscious self is that part of self that is Not-Known and is Un-Known that it is not known. **It is the deep memories of the soul's history and incarnations as human and non-human. Referred to as the akashic records**. This part of self may be experienced as separate from self. As an entity, Guardian at the Gate or the Dweller on the Threshold. The un-conscious mind is accessed through Divine Understanding from the Sacred Heart knowing or inner communion with the cells and DNA of the human vessel. The unconsciousness mind binds the soul to trauma and illusionary matrix of fear and limitation, until cleared through free-will and choice as a sovereign being. It is the Reptilian Brain. The unconsciousness mind is transformed through conscious awareness and plays a role in the raising of the Kundalini in the process of enlightenment.

Our **Higher-Self** may be thought of as source energy spiraling down through our sacred heart knowing. Father Spirit as Divine Intelligence. The Sacred Fire of Spirit. Masculine symbol of downward triangle. The Light-Self.

Our **Soul-Self** may be thought of as source energy spiraling up through our sacred heart knowing.

Mother Spirit as Divine Intelligence. The Sacred Fire of Matter. Feminine symbol of the upwards triangle. The Shadow-Self.

Our **Empowered Co-Creator Self** may be thought of as being a God Goddess in human form. Unified Intelligence of higher-self and soul-self, light and shadow, team-light and team-dark. The Sacred Fire of Solar Sun in Crystalline Human Form. The symbol of the triangles merged as one

Star Merkaba. Peace as an eternal Golden Being of Unlimited Potential in temporary human form.

Our Soul experiences every moment of life, as the Watcher of Self, recording the memories. When the experience is painful or traumatic, the soul will recognize this experience as not matching what is known within as spiritual truth. An inner process of assessment is made to protect self. The inner **Self-Governing Structure** may take an action as a self-defense mechanism which over time binds the soul and self to limitation. The assessment and action we take is stored in the unconscious or subconscious part of our being as a soul level agreement, or contract. Our physical body holds the space of these energetic contracts. Soul level contracts and vows may be held in the cellular memory, the RNA & DNA and in the etheric templates referred to as the akashic records. The same is true for our past lives. These are all part of our multidimensional-selves as an eternal being in temporary human form.

The memories stored in the sub-conscious and unconscious mind are dense outdated energetics causing what they are to manifest in the outer reality as chaos, war, strife, poverty, limitation, illness, limitation, victim consciousness and many more records of suffering. Experienced at in the collective consciousness as world and global strife.

Earth is now in a higher frequency and dimension, allowing agreements and contracts created during a third dimensional awareness to be easily transmuted and rescinded through heart centered consciousness. Each individual who steps into the fifth dimensional world of being and activating the Divine Plan is adding to the collective clearing of the collective global soul records of Mother Earth as a Sentient Being of One. When a group of individuals unify through one sacred intent in meditation, prayer, song or sacred vibration the clearing and transmuting of the collective soul-records is exponential creating waves of freedom and liberation for the many and give birth to Heaven on Earth, Just for Being.

AFFIRMATIONS

An affirmation is a statement of fact or assertion, usually stated from a place of belief or acceptance. It is to declare ones support for, uphold or defend, to accept or confirm, to give a sense of value too. Firm is from the Latin word to make "firm" or into form. An affirmation is a way of cognizing the outcome we choose to create or experience.

The Unity Church defines affirmative prayers as a way, "to state the Truth, even in the face of contrary evidence." This means if you are sick, you affirm health. If you are poor, you affirm prosperity; if you are confused, you affirm guidance, etc. The idea is to affirm the divinely intended Truth verses less than intended experience truth. In other words **to affirm is to decree the Highest Intended Idea in every situation.**

The second and equally important step in affirmative prayer is to invite the presence of Source within self to speak the Word. It is the spirit of God, Divine Intelligence or Source Energy within who prays, talks, breaths, listens, takes action and affirms. As I AM God Goddess in human form, working through human form and healing through human form. It's surrendering to your higher Self and giving it Voice. It is not the individual's talent, book, project or artwork. It is Spirit, Source within through divine understanding that co-creates the book, project, artwork or action through human BEING.

The restoral of "Sacred Trust" happens as each human Being trusts the reception of divine guidance through divine understanding and then takes action on this knowing by setting ones intent and following through with aligned action. The reception of understanding is feminine in nature. The action of setting intent and follow through with aligned action is masculine in nature. The Being is God Goddess in human form.

The feminine negative polarity receives the Divine Plan through inner knowing. The masculine positive polarity takes action to fulfill the Divine Plan. The Being discerns through inner wisdom and divine understanding. It is important to allow the rational mind to know the sacred desire of the sacred heart and to take action through intent and divine alignment to manifest or out-picture this desire. For many individuals the rational mind is hiding the sacred desire from the sacred heart to keep the individual safe. This hiding served in the moment of past however they now hide from the self the joy and pleasure and intended for the being. The hiding of ones sacred desire from the sacred heart manifests in life as the core wound of betrayal and abandonment.

The violet flame is the spiritual solvent that clears unconscious energetics of betrayal, separation dis-trust, pain and suffering. The violet flame is the balance of the pink receptive flame of love and the blue active flame of power. Through the golden flame of understanding humans are birthing their golden self and the golden age of enlightenment.

THREE-FOLD FORMULAS FOR MANIFESTATION

Transcending Duality through the Unified One Heart.

By placing your hand on your Sacred Heart while Affirming Out-Loud, one automatically drops the mind through the heart connecting and unifying the polarities of duality. This is much like connecting the positive and negative side of a battery to turn on the current, or in this case the life source of divine Fohat. With a hand on the Sacred Heart begin to decree, and proclaim out loud the desired intent through the Throat Center of Creative Active Intelligence.

The First Three Rays of God.

Ray 1. Divine Will and Power, anchors and is activated in the Crown as Divine Mind.
Blue active flame of power, right side of sacred heart and body.

Ray 2. Divine Love and Wisdom, anchors and is activated in the Sacred Heart as Divine Love.
Pink receptive flame of love and understanding, left side of sacred heart and body.

Ray 3. Divine Creative Active Intelligence, anchors and is activated in the Throat as Co-Creator.

Golden flame of Sacred Being as God Goddess co-creating the divine plan, through the balance of love, power and understanding, With Ease, JUST FOR BEING. In the now... Center of sacred heart and body.

Humans as co-creator Beings, are the Word of God. We are here to be the empowered individualized expressions of our god goddess selves. We are angels in human form and we have dominion over the spirit realm, including both the Angelic and Elemental kingdoms.

1. Placing a Hand on the Heart automatically connects the positive and negative polarities of the mind and heart, much like a copper wire connecting the two sides of a battery.
   a. The Mind being the place where the First Ray of God anchors, The Heart being the place where the Second Ray of God anchors. Balancing Power, Love and Understanding.

2. Then Speak OUTLOUD. We create through the power of the spoken word.
   a. The Throat is the place where the Third Ray of God anchors (Creative Active Intelligence).

3. Begin to say out loud, *"My Higher-Self now resides in me".*
   a. Imagine a Golden Orb of Light from your God Self or the God Head, descending into the Sacred Heart

4. Continue speaking aloud," ***Divine Understanding is now activated in me. I Claim my birthright to KNOW, HEAR, and SEE as God Goddess, as Spirit does. I take back my power to Know, See and Hear as God & Goddess does, through my own Sacred Heart, my own Knowing and my own Understanding. I ask my Soul and Higher-Self to be with me today and always. I thank my Soul and Higher-Self for answering all my questions and for showing me my Divine Pathway. I ask this knowledge and guidance to be PHYSICALLY DEMONSTRATED,***

CLEARLY REVEALED, PLACED IN FROM OF ME, "I ASK GOD FOR THE BURNING BUSH".

It is through Higher-Self in the Sacred Heart that we can know the answers to all our questions and have our Divine Path revealed through us. It is Our Birthright to Know as God does and to be Divinely Guided. When we ask our Higher-Self or Source a question from our Sacred Heart an answer is always provided. This answer is in the language of the Soul. The Language of the soul is Symbols, Coincidence, Synchronicity and Metaphor. In the beginning it may take a few hours or days to have an answer revealed. A coincidence two or more times is considered a message. It is important to open to trusting the **ON BOARD DIVINE GUIDANCE SYSTEM** held in the sacred heart. Practicing using the body pendulum or muscle testing to confirm guidance is recommended.

> *I invite my Soul-Self and Higher-Self to be HERE, and now clearly reveal through my own understanding and knowing all the ANSWERS that I now ask.*

Muscle Testing: Trusting Self and Divine Guidance.

Exercise: Body Pendulum: Learn about the body pendulum and begin to practice muscle testing to discern it for yourself. Place your hand on your heart and ask your body to show you YES. Do not lock your knees; your body will naturally sway towards one direction, usually towards the front. Now ask your body to show you NO, usually you will sway to the rear. Now ask your body a question such as "my name is_____". Let your body answer through the sway. If your sway does not move forward and back, then learn to balance your chakras and it will begin to do so. You can also utilize muscle testing, or any other form of kinesiology to discern truth. Try it, it works!

The body pendulum will seem to not work: When the self does not trust self, such as the mind not trusting the heart or body. When the human is bound to being in the body, on earth or in relationship is painful. When the chakras are shut down or out of balance.

It is an inherent right as an eternal being in temporary incarnated form to be free and have the Divine Understanding of Source activated and known from within the Sacred Heart. Therefore when one places their **hand over their heart and speak out-loud through the power of the spoken word** the following affirmations a shift is often experienced.

> *"I AM open to trusting my body pendulum in the now"*

> *"I Claim Sacred Trust and am open to the body pendulum showing me truth for my good."*

> *"I thank my body pendulum for working in the now, I thank my body and mind for trusting my body pendulum."*

> *"I AM open to Source Demonstrating Truth through my sacred-heart body pendulum."*

The body pendulum is a form of dowsing or kinesiology. It is recommended that each individual begin to practice different forms of muscle testing and dowsing to strengthen ones trust in the On Board Guidance System of the Sacred Heart Knowing. The Higher-Self will always answer any question requested through the sacred heart center. Dowsing is one way to become aware of these answers and divine guidance. The process of using the body pendulum or muscle testing creates a bridge of trust between the rational reasoning mind sometimes called ego, and the intuitive intelligent mind sometimes called instinct. When the Higher-Self is invited to reside in the driver's seat of our Self Governing Structure, the On-Board Guidance System of Sacred-Heart builds the bridge between mind and emotion, the inner feminine and the inner masculine, duality and separation, unifying the multi-dimensional being and experience. As trust of conscious awareness expands the mind is ready to grasp the cosmic history of our original soul's origins in multiple incarnated forms. The Body Pendulum allows the answers to come with ease during the clearing process of Divine Revelation.

Affirming through the Three-Fold Formula.

A Three-Fold Formula for Co-Creation utilizes a consistent formula of three affirmations to release, choose again, and magnify or magnetically attract the new experience. Creating the new momentum that now rolls forward manifesting in form that word spoken into form. This formula works through the sacred science of the Sacred Trinity.

1. Rescind and Release that which no longer serves, making a space or spiritual vacuum. This is the equivalent of clearing out clutter in your home. It is difficult to put new clothing in a full closet. The clutter of old agreements and unconscious or unprocessed emotions stored in the cellular memories keep the individual from anchoring the light body. Many individuals are storing their parents and or other people's emotions in the emotional causal body. Many individuals are storing their parents or authoritative people's thoughts in the mental causal body. Many individuals are storing traumatic wounds of self and others in the etheric casual body. Some individuals were born into this life with wounded blueprints. These wounded blueprints may be referred to as misaims.

2. Choose again by claiming in the now or being open to experience the divine in form. Conscious choice is a gift and the key for each individual to become empowered and begin to co-create the new paradigm of heaven on earth or to experience fulfilling life. In choosing the new, it is important to be open to receiving the good one is intended to have. The individual must be open to letting go of the past and open the hands or self to receive and accept the new. Each time a new choice is made, any unconscious agreement against this choice, will be brought to the surface of awareness. This may happen through somatic symptoms or in the outer manifestation and projection of experiences in the environment or with people.

3. Magnify, by focusing on the divine intent often through repetitive affirmations, declaration, and declaring this to be the only chosen experience in the now and future. Whatever intent, thought, or frequency an individual focuses on is like a magnet and magnetically draws towards it the manifested equivalent. The subconscious is programmed by each individual's thoughts and daily focus. Without conscious awareness the individual's subconscious will become muddied and manifest chaos. Through deliberate conscious intent and awareness the subconscious becomes a crystalline vehicle allowing the quickened physical manifestation of each sacred intent or decree. An analogy may be drawn from Dr. Masiru Emoto's work on the research with water. Creative expression, such as writing, drawing, dance and moving is a powerful way to magnify a sacred intent. Vision Boarding and journaling with affirmations activate and program the subconscious to magnetically manifest. Getting all of the senses involved also empowers the manifestation of the intent. Conscious daily reminders such as wearing a ring or piece of jewelry, may remind one of the desired intent. In some ways one must complete the karmic equation of out vibrating the previous programing.

Karmic Equation: Repetitive, *positive self-empowering thoughts* = **must equal and out vibrate**= *negative self-limiting thoughts.*

RESCIND & RELEASE Affirmation

The rescind and release affirmation empowers us to un-create and let go of any energetics that no longer serve us. It is our Birthright and our inherent co-creator power to transmute, undo, forgive, release, rescind, delete, cancel or un-create or transmute all that no longer serves us, blocks our divine good or is not of love. This creates a spiritual vacuum or empty space for the newly chosen to manifest.

1.   **Rescind and Release:** Release any mental beliefs, assessments, structures, rules, should or anything else that no longer serves you. Most often we are releasing the Mental Body, or Human Mind of all the thoughts and believes we choose to be safe in the Third Dimensional World. They served us perfectly when we choose and now have become our limitations. **Place your hand on your sacred heart and speak out loud.**

"I undo, rescind, rewind, delete, withdraw, let go, forgive, cancel, cast out, banish, release......

*"I release all soul level contracts, for all lifetimes that may be stored a,
in my being both conscious and unconscious. I now choose to release tha,
to try harder and work harder for my good."*

"I now release all agreements that life is hard".

"I allow myself and am open to letting go"

*"I release all judgment and condemnation of myself, everyone, everywhere, and
everything for all time" "I release that I must wait for my Good."*

These are examples of rescind and release affirmations. Take some time
to identify self- governing structures, mental thought patterns, habits and
spiritual contracts that no longer serve the Divinely Intended Good of
Higher-Self in temple form. Begin to rescind these agreements through
written and spoken affirmations. Remember to place one hand on your
heart space when Speaking Out-Loud to unify heart and mind as truth
of one love.

NOW, ALLOW or OPEN Affirmations.

Many people have heard about affirmations and know of the Now
affirmation. The now affirmation states a thought form as happening in
the Now. "I now Forgive". The allow affirmation or I am open affirmation,
moves past any soul level agreement that might veto the now affirmation.
The I am open or I allow affirmation, creates a bridge from the undesired
experience to manifesting the Divinely Intended desire. "I allow Forgiveness
into my life." "I open myself to experience"

2.   **Invoke:** Claim, Allow or Open yourself to receive that which you
desire, is for your highest good, or is as God Goddess would create. **Place
your hand on your sacred heart and speak out loud.**

*"I claim my Sacred Birthrights, Eternal Peace & Freedom, Infinite Love &
Supply, and Sacred Truth in Knowing & Understanding as God Goddess or
my Higher Self does.*

"I claim my divine birthright to receive infinite love, infinite supply, acceptance, money, abundance, freedom, prosperity, acknowledgement, assistance, divine good, joy, laughter, worthiness, success, appreciation, cash, donations, gifts, opportunities, choices, financial freedom."

"I claim my divine birthright to experience eternal peace, wisdom, acceptance, freedom, pleasure, laughter, prosperity, community, fellowship, companionship, unity, balance, justice, harmony."

"I claim my divine birthright to know as god goddess knows, to stand in my light, to know divine truth to know the way, to be the way, to fulfill my divine purpose and re-claim all my divinely intended birthrights".

"I Claim Easy Life as my Birthright, I am Open to easy, and I allow myself to experience all the Easy Life that Spirit intends me to have. If it is Gods will that I have an Easy Life, I now am open and choose Easy Life"

"I Claim FREEDOM as my Birthright." "I Claim my Sacred Being."

"I Claim my Right to Exist, I Claim my Sacred Space, my Sacred Value."

"I take Back my Divinely Intended Power. I Claim my Power to be a Creator-Being"

"I now choose to invoke my Divinely Intended Birthrights"

"If it is Gods Will that I have the Power to be a Co-Creator Being, then I allow it"

"I Now Declare than Only Divine Order resides in me, everyone, everywhere and everything."

"I claim my success today and every day, I claim my good today and every day. I claim Victory in this process!"

These are examples of Now, Allow and Open affirmations. Take some time to identify divinely intended desires of the sacred heart. Be open to receiving this Divine Good in the Now. Begin to allow oneself to experience this good in the now, just for affirming it while being incarnated in form. Claim the desired good as happening in the now, with ease and just for being through written and spoken affirmations. Remember to place one hand on your heart space when Speaking Out-Loud to unify heart and mind as truth of one love.

3.   **Magnify:** Set yourself up for success, by being the magnet of your desire. Imagine, envision, speak and be the action of your desired outcome. Choose with Deliberate Intent what you invoke, intend, and focus your energy on 24/7, as a conscious being.

Place your hand on your sacred heart and speak out loud.

"I now only draw towards me life, people, situations and events that FREE me!"

"I now only draw towards me life, people, situations and events that are Easy!"

"I now only draw toward me relationships and life that are for my Highest Good."

"I Choose Love today, I Choose Joy today, I Choose Easy today"

"I imagine and envision the outcome that is for my Highest Good"

"I walk in Perfect Timing with the Universe, I Am at the right place at the right time. All timing is Divinely Ordered in my Life, I only draw towards me people, situations, life, and events that are Divinely Ordered and in Divine Timing"

These are examples choosing what one wants to experience in life by being the vibration of the choice. Take some time to identify divinely intended desires of the sacred heart. Include the five known senses in the manifesting process. Create written and spoken affirmations add visuals and self-care reminders to sustain the sacred intent in vibration. Imagine, envision and visualize this good. Add song, chanting, toning, oils and movement. Create Vision Boards, Lists, Journals and group meditation circles. Remember to place one hand on your heart when affirming out-loud, for the Power of the Spoken Word to Manifest through the Unified Heart and Mind with Ease.

Example Three-Fold Formula for Co-Creation:

Place your hand on your Sacred Heart and Speak Out-Loud through the Power of the Spoken Word.

"I rescind any soul level contract, vow, agreement, or pact that I have ever made in this life time or any life time, human and non-human that: (fill in blank) _____."

"I Now Command these energetics' to clear from my conscious and un-conscious memories including my akashic records, cellular memories, causal bodies and etheric blue print."

"Placing them into the Violet Flame to clear the memories, records, cause, core and effect for all lifetimes."

"I CLAIM and take back my Inherent Birthright to be FREE.

I Claim Freedom and Sovereignty as my Birthright!"

"I Claim and take back my inherent Birthright's to have CHOICE and FREE WILL."

"L NOW CHOOSE to Create a New Reality!"

"I NOW CHOOSE to create, (fill in Blank) _____."

"From this day forward, I only draw towards me, people, situations, or events that are of LOVING SAFE AND TRUSTWORTHY, and are: (fill in blank) _____."

"Anything that is not this Choice is now banished from my life!!!"

"Only DIVINE ORDER now exists in my Mind in my Body, in my Relationships and in my Life!

I AM CONNECTED!! I DO BELONG!!"

"These sacred decrees or something better now manifests in form for the good that is the highest for all".

Conscious Co-Creation Formulas for Success:

Sacred Trust: Trust in self, Trust in Spirit, Trust in Life, and Trust in relationships. Open yourself to Trust that you are a powerful creator being, who is sacred, loved and worthy Just for Being! You have never done anything wrong and you never will. God is You! You are an Unlimited Infinite Co-Creator Being. An eternal being in temporary human form. Immortal. All life is an opportunity to experience individuation of your Divinity. You do not have to know how to Trust or Believe, just be open to it. Your Higher Self will do the rest. **Place hand on Heart and speak out loud.**

"God I do not know who to trust, but I am open to experiencing Sacred Trust. If it is God's Divine Will, I Claim Sacred Trust as my Divine Birthright! I now only Draw to me people situations, and events that are safe and trustworthy. Please physically demonstrate sacred trust to me."

"I Claim Sacred Trust as my inherent right and reality. I now only draw to me trustworthy people, situations and events"

"Thank you Higher-Self for the trustworthy relationships, and life I experience today."

"Sacred Trust is activated and now resides in this situation."

"I Am open to trusting myself and others."

DIVINE WILL: Align with the Will of God or your Higher Self. "Not my will but GOD'S WILL now resides in me, my life, and this relationship."

"If it is God's will that I have power, I co-create, I am Love, I am Light, I AM worthy, I AM Sacred, then I open myself and Allow myself to BE it." Choice equals Will! To Choose is to Will. **Place hand on Heart and speak out loud.**

"I am now divinely aligned with the will of God. Not my lower human will but Divine Will now resides in me and my life. Divine Choices are now made known to me. I choose for the highest good with ease."

"I am now divinely aligned with my Higher-Self Source energy and the one unified heart."

"The will of higher-self now does its perfect work in and through me and my life today."

Protection: IT IS SAFE! Take back your Birthright of Divine Safety, Security and Stability. "Thank you God for directing me", Thank you God for protecting me. Invite all fear and mistrust into love. "I invite the part of me that is in fear into love that part of me does not know love and has served me perfectly by teaching me to be safe. I thank all my Angels and Guides for now escorting all Fear into Love. **Place hand on Heart and speak out loud.**

"I Claim Divine Safety and Protection as my Birthright. I now only draw to me people, situations, and events where I experience being Safe and Protected."

"I am open to experiencing Safety."

"I send my higher-self out ahead of me to only bring forth safe life."

Forgive: Begin to forgive all painful experiences from your past. Let go of judgment and condemnation of self, everyone, everywhere and everything for all times. Again you do not have to know how, just be open to it. **Place hand on Heart and speak out loud.**

"I do not know how or where I most need Forgiveness; I AM open to Divine Forgiveness."

"I Claim Eternal Forgiveness as my Divine Birthright. I ask the angels to send this forgiveness back to me through this and all lifetimes human and non-human."

"I am eternally forgiven with ease."

"Thank you Spirit and Higher-Self for the physical demonstration and experience of forgiveness in my life today and every day."

Unify: Move out of the duality of the third dimensional world by stepping into the Unified Multi- dimensional world. Begin to pair all judgment and limiting thoughts and beliefs with the polarized good. Observe oneself 24/7 becoming aware of any repeated thought, feeling, or belief and begin to pair each negative or less than experience with the Highest Divinely Intended Form, or desire. Recognize your multidimensionality you are a Cosmic Being experiencing multiple realities at once. **Place hand on Heart and speak out loud.**

"Only Divine Order and the Healing Love of Spirit now reside here."

"All is unified and aligned in my life with ease."

"The Unified Good is now Activated and Resides here."

Power of the One: Unified through the One Heart of Truth. The wound of being separate from God keeps the individual separate from the divinely intended. Life experiences of being different, ugly and less than others is manifested. Each soul's unique individuality allows God Goddess to express self as its own color of the rainbow. Human spelled as HUE-Man, each individual is separate hue and all hues or colors form the one white light of Spirit. Separation from Spirit leads to fear. Fear divides humans while love unifies humans. **Place hand on Heart and speak out loud.**

"I Claim the Power of the ONE, my one Unique Individualized Expression of my God/Goddess, my own Hue, frequency or color of the Rainbow. All hues, hue-mans are now Unified through the One Rainbow Fire."

103

"The Sacred White-Fire of Fohat the Divine Life-Source is Activated and Restored in this ONE moment."

"I am my ONE highest divinely intended purified expression of god goddess in human form."

"I am Unified through the Power of the ONE HEART."

"Through the Power of the One Unified Heart in Me, Infinite options solutions, answers, ways, and choices are now lined up in front of me, demonstrating themselves.

"Through the Power of the One, I now KNOW the ONE choice to choose in the ONE moment I choose, that is for the One Unified Good."

Commune: Mighty I AM. Send your Mighty I Am Presence, you Higher Self out ahead of you. Commune with your Higher Self by sharing your hearts desires, your visions, needs, fears, etc.… This is the higher self that is one with the one unified heart. **Place hand on Heart and speak out loud.**

"Thank you higher self for going out ahead to remove all obstacles, clear the way, and meet all my needs both known and unknown." "Thank you Higher Self for taking care of this situation ahead of me."

"I Send my Mighty I AM presence out ahead of me to remove all obstacles, fear, density and blockages and to take care of all my Divine Needs both known and unknown, prior to me getting there."

Pleasure: It is our Birthright to experience Sacred Pleasure in Physical Form. All guilt, resentment, anger, shame, embarrassment, remorse, fear, and blame will keep us from our highest good and joy. Allow pleasure… **Place hand on Heart and speak out loud.**

"My mind pleases me, my body pleases me, my thoughts please me, my words please me, my family pleases me, my relationships please me, my home pleases me, my job pleases me, my life pleases me, and everyone, everything and

everywhere now please me. I only draw towards me divine pleasure." **Repeat the same affirmation with the word FREE's and FREEDOM.**

"I Claim Sacred Pleasure as my Birthright! My mind now pleases me, my body pleases me, my emotions please me, my friends and family pleases me. My work pleases me, my car pleases me, my bills please me, my life pleases me, everyone, everywhere and everything now please me. I AM PLEASED!"

"I Claim Freedom as my Birthright! My mind now frees me, my body frees me, my emotions free me, my past frees me, my present frees me, my future frees me, everyone, everywhere and everything now frees me. My family and friends free me. I AM FREE.".

Consciousness of Abundance and Infinite Supply.

Whatever one knows as their inner most desire from the sacred heart as the possibility of what it would be like in Heaven or a Utopian world. Can be manifested in form with ease through sacred intention using sacred science of manifestation. There is an infinite supply of light in the celestial realm and material resources is the Devic Realm or Divine Mother/Matter.

Mother Earth loves to share her natural resources with those who accept their stewardship as co-creators of the Divine Plan on Earth. The key here is reverence. When Mother Earth, the Devic Realm is honored through prayer, request and proper use of her resources. She will give freely. Mother Earth's resources include everything in the physical and used by humans and animals for thriving while incarnated in form on the Earth Plane. These include plants, crystals, minerals, trees, water, air, food, shelter, and all forms of nourishment. Some indigenous peoples teach to leave Mother Earth tobacco as a sacred offering for her blessings. Some religions teach to bless each meal. These are examples of Divine Reverence that bring forth harmony in nature and human life.

Money. Money is the token of the rich substance of matter. It is the representation of the Divine Source as unlimited. Money is the substance that represents an exchange of energy. Money is Energy. Source is Energy.

Humans are Energy. There is an infinite supply of energy and in infinite supply of money.

Those individuals who are bound to a belief that money is evil, or corrupt with experience these circumstances with money. Those who hate money or think there is not enough money will experience hatred and not enough money.

As money is energy, humans can choose to create abundance and the experience of having enough by shifting their cognitive belief systems and choosing to love money as energy. Choosing to love self as energy and choosing to love Spirit as energy.

Money is a stepped down currency from gold. It is a paper substitute. For some people working with the color gold increases prosperity where green may not be as successful. For others working with the ruby red ray of the life force will help one to experience the fullness of life and life's intended resources.

> *I open myself to receive all the tangible good, intended for me in the forms of money, cash, income, wealth, riches, gold and abundance of divine resources.*

> *I am open to loving money, I love money, and Money loves me.*

> *I claim the rich substance intended for me.*

Gold. Gold is the original currency and is the mineral that is activated in the human blood when the human chooses to be light and activates the solar light body. The science of alchemy sought to turn lead into gold. This is the analogy of the soul's transformative process of becoming the Golden Being in the Golden Age of Enlightenment.

Gold has recently been scientifically found to heal and transmute radiation. Gold is what the Niberians from the planet Niberu were mining on earth to repair that planets damaged atmosphere. The greed for gold has caused the human history to be one of slavery, oppression and despair.

If one had to hide gold in previous life-times then ones gold may be hidden from the self in the now.

If one enslaved others or was enslaved for gold, they may carry heavy karma to clear the soul's records with gold and other earth minerals or resources.

Some mystery schools teach that when the 2nd ray of Spirit, the Golden ray of Love and Understanding, and the 5th ray of Spirit, the ray of concrete and abstract knowledge (science and spirituality), are unified, the Earth will again have abundant gold flowing through her veins.

This is the GOLDEN AGE OF ENLIGHTENMENT. Each individual is ready to become a Golden Sun in human form as an Eternal Being in Temporary human form.

I claim the golden way, I claim my golden being. I clam the golden age of enlightenment.

I open myself to have all the gold intended for me. Gold is revealed to me.

VIOLET FLAME DECREES AND TRANSMUTATION.

The violet ray as the seventh ray of spirit is the flame of freedom, transmutation, continuous daily self-care rituals and spiritual mastery. It is the perfect balance of the pink flame of love and the blue flame of power. The violet flame is the balance of the masculine positive and feminine negative polarities.

Ultra-Violet light is used in industry to purify both water and air. Backpackers can purchase a battery powered 'steripen" that can purify water with ultraviolet light.

It is helpful to vocalize violet flame decrees, routinely to dissolve negativity, fear, struggle, conflict and karmic debt. An example is choosing to chant violet flame decrees for seven minutes a day. Since the seventh ray is the ray of mastery and continuous self-care ritual, developing a personal self-care routine with the violet flame will increase self-mastery while decreasing struggle. In the beginning working with the violet flame will bring up the dense energetics that are ready to be acknowledged and transmuted. Over time the souls records are purified increasing the individuals light quotient, frequency and tolerance for the activation of the sacred white fire at the center of each atom. With forward momentum the individual may not need to work with the violet flame as frequently. When life becomes difficult or dense it is easy to begin a more deliberate focused intent and chant violet flame decrees for several hours until the inner self senses a shift back into peace.

Violet Flame Decree's

Remember to place your hand on the Sacred Heart and Decree Out loud.

> *"I AM A BEING OF VIOLET FIRE" "I AM THE PURITY GOD DESIRES"*…. Repeat in chant. Replace with words such as "My home is a home of violet fire, It is the purity Spirit desires. My life is a life of violet fire, it's the Life Spirit desires. My work is the work of the violet fire it is the purity spirt desires. Continue chanting….

> *Fill in the blank,"* _____*is a being of violet fire. Fill in the blank,* _____*is the purity Spirit desires".*

> *"I AM THE VIOLET FLAME IN ME BURNING OUT OF PURITY!"* repeat in chant. Make up your own violet flame chants…

When the individual begins to invoke and work with the violet flame, unconscious energetics begin to come from the unknown into the known part of being. This may stir up repressed emotions, experiences and energetics to be cleared and removed from the soul records. The energetic records are sometimes referred to as the dross of karmic debt. As the records are cleared permanently it makes an energetic space or void in the individual. Therefore it is important to decree, or declare what the individual desires in its place. By identifying the Divinely Intended Idea and speaking or affirming it into Form.

The first ray of Spirit is the Sapphire Blue Ray of Divine Protection and Purpose. This ray appears as the sacred white fire in the spiritual octaves and as Sapphire Blue in the octaves of matter.

The first ray of Spirit in the octaves of Spirit is the Ray of Archangel Michael and Archia Faith.

The **fourth Ray of Spirit** in the octaves of matter is the **Ray of the Elohim Purity and Astrea.** The Ray is the Ascension Flame "Shakti" activated in the root chakra. It is the kundalini, vital life source of matter.

The Elohim as the builders of form bind the molecular level. This invocation clears the matter of toxins and begins to purify matter or form. This is the caduceus action of the Sacred White Fire.

In life where one is intending to be free and remain pure of low vibrating energetics it is good to first invoke divine protection. Before the daily routine of violet flame work it is helpful to invoke divine protection. The Elohim and Archangels are waiting to be called on by the human co-creator so they can being the work of co-creating hand in hand the divine plan on earth.

PROTECTION DECREEE's

Invoke Divine Protection.

> *I call forth Archangel Michael and his legions of blue light for divine protection and the ability to cut through all obstructions.*

> *"I Invoke the Elohim of the Fourth Ray, the Ascension Flame, Purity & Astrea. I surround myself, house, space, building, community with the white fire of Purity and the Blue Fire of Astrea."*

Envision two concentric circles of fire blazing light zig zagging around the waist or center. Envision the Blue Sword of Astrea piercing up through the center. This will snap off or de-magnify the miss-qualified parasitic entities bound to the molecular levels. This invocation may only provide 24 hour or short term freedom. Allowing one to utilize the Violet Flame for permanent freedom.

Violet Flame guides of the Seventh Ray of freedom, mastery and transmutation. If one likes they can invoke and call forth assistance from the Violet Ray Guides who are as follows. One can also work with the violet flam without calling these individual guides. Some find comfort in establishing a connection with the spiritual real through these individualized aspects of Divine Intelligence known as Source of God.

Archangels, Zadekial & Holy Amethyst. Celestial Realm.

Elohim, Arcturus & Victoria. Devic Realm.

Ascended Masters, Saint Germaine and Lady Portia. Sons and Daughters of God as God and Goddess. Christed Beings that humans are intended to be.

> *"I call forth St. Germaine, Archangel Zadekial, Holy Amethyst, Arcturus, Cosmic Victory and all Violet Ray Beings. Or I call forth Divine Assistance and Purity of the Violet Ray.*

Consciously choose to direct the violet flame sending it into the past and every aspect of the multi-dimensional being both known and unknown.

> *The violet flame fills my being; every molecule, particle and atom of my being is now filled with the violet flame. The violet flame fills me, moves through me and surrounds me. The violet flame fills and moves into my unconsciousness, sub-consciousness, consciousness, all my causal bodies and my aura. The violet flame moves into and fills my past, for this lifetime, all past life times and future lifetimes.*

The violet flame fills and surrounds my home, business and all of my life. The violet flame now fills and surrounds all of my family and our friends and loved ones. The violet flame now fills and surrounds my town, the state, the country, and the Earth. The violet flame now transmutes and frees me from all karmic debt.

List energetics to be placed in the violet flame as they become conscious to self.

I place_____ (all emotional, traumatic, less than, and karmic experiences) into the violet flame, to TRANSMUTE and CLEAR THE MEMEORY, RECORD, CAUSE, CORE, and EFFECT, FOR ALL LIFETIMES,

The Elementals bind the karmic or unwanted experience into place at the molecular level. Command and give permission to the elementals who are bound to the karmic or unwanted energy to be free.

I Give permission too, and thank the elemental beings, (builders of form) for releasing and letting go of all miss-qualified or miss-created forms and being brought forth into their current highest divinely intended purified form in the now.

Be open to experience forgiveness and freedom. Especially in the unknown places of hardened energetics.

I Claim my divine birthright to experience; DIVINE FORGIVENESS, FREEDOM, LIBERTY, JUSTICE, OPPORTUNITIES & MERCY today and every day.

Claim, Invoke allow and be open to Success and Victory in the Now and every day. Each time the being asks for success and victory in the now. Source immediately responds by putting down these experiences.

I CLAIM VICTORY in this process! With Mighty Victory I Am now Free and Liberated. I AM Light, I AM Love, And I AM Free!! I AM ASCENDED"

The violet flame is the spiritual solvent that purifies the soul's records by transmuting dense planes into lighter planes of the Divinely Intended Plan. The Universe as Divine Intelligence is conspiring to empower, support, free and transform the awakened human who is choosing to co-create in accompaniment with the Octaves of Light known as the spiritual hierarchy through the plane of the transcended, un-manifest and manifested dimensions.

IMMACULATE CONCEPT. Hold a place of purity for an on behalf of our brothers and sisters of light. Activate the Divinely Intended Plan to co-create the new. The Divinely Intended Plan is known in part as the Virtues of the Solar Hierarchy or God.

Traditionally it has been instructed that the Ascended Masters, Angels, and Divine Mother hold a place of purity for and on behalf of humanity. Divine Mother has informed me that she will work for and on behalf of every human who chooses to practice the act of holding the immaculate concept or flame of purity for and behalf of all sentient beings. Humans as Crystalline Light Beings choosing to co-create Heaven on Earth can free humans and all elementals of miss qualified forms.

CREATING HEAVEN ON EARTH THROUGH THE IMMACULATE CONCEPT

Only Love Is Real

Standing in my Divinity, as my Higher-Self, I now choose to hold thoughts of purity and love for and on behalf of family, my friends, mankind and myself. I choose to practice the act of the "IMMACULATE CONCEPT".

In this process whenever I experience fear or undesirable qualities in a friend, family or situation, I recognize this situation and hold beside it, pure thoughts of what I would like to experience, or what God sees as the divinely intended idea, blueprint, or possibility. To do this I open myself to see as God Sees. Thus activating my Divine Understanding of each situation I am involved in. I begin to declare with the Power of the Spoken Word this Divine Awareness by speaking out loud the "Immaculate Concept" for each situation.

Place Hand on Sacred Heart and Speak out loud through the power of the spoken word. Fill in each blank with the name of person or situation and of self, add additional Divine Concepts for each situation as Divinely Intended.

THE POWER OF DIVINE LOVE, (ETERNAL TRANSFIGURING LOVE) IS NOW ACTIVATED IN ME, IN _____ AND IN OUR RELATIONSHIP.

GODS PERFECT LOVE NOW DOES ITS PERFECT WORK IN AND THROUGH_____.

ONLY GODS HEALING LOVE WORKS IN AND THROUGH_____, IN AND THROUGH ME, AND IN AND THROUGH OUR RELATIONSHIP!

ONLY DIVINE ORDER EXHISTS IN__(NAME)_____, ONLY DIVINE ORDER EXHIST IN ME. ONLY DIVINE ORDER NOW RESIDES IN OUR RELATIONSHIP.

GODS WILL, POWER & PERFECTION NOW RESIDES AND WORKS IN_____,

THE PROSPERING POWER OF GODS INFINATE SUPPLY IS NOW DEMONSTRATED IN AND THROUGH_____.

DIVINE PEACE AND HARMONY NOW RESIDE IN _____. ALL IS BALANCED THROUGH THE INDWELLING OF THE CHRST, OR THE HOLY SPIRIT.

GODS INFINATE WISDOM IS NOW ACTIVATED IN THE HEART OF THIS MATTER. DIVINE UNDERSTANDING IS ACTIVATED IN ME, IN _____ AND IN OUR RELATIONSHIP.

THE HEALING LOVE OF GOD NOW RESIDES IN ME AND FLOWS THROUGH ME, MY HEART AND MY HANDS. EVERYTHING I TOUCH IS NOW BLESSED WITH THE HEALING LOVE OF GOD.

ALL THAT IS HIDDEN IS NOW REVEALED THROUGH GODS LIGHT. DIVINE TRUTH & ILUMINATION IS ACTIVATED HERE AND NOW REVEALS THE WAY!

DIVINE PURITY, RESTORATION & RESSURECTION NOW RESIDE HERE. DIVINE JUSTICE, FAIRNESS & VITORY NOW RESIDE IN THIS SITUATION.

GODS DIVINE ETERNAL FORGIVENESS AND MERCY NOW RESIDE IN ME AND IN _____.

~only love is real~

ONLY LOVE IS REAL: Realize that anyone in your life who mistreats or behaves from a place of anger, jealousy, fear, or other dense emotion, is a Being in Pain. This person needs more love not less. As a Co-Creator Being you can choose to hold a space of LOVE for this person. **Place hand on Heart and speak out loud.**

"Only the Healing Love of God now activated and resides in this person, their life, and our relationship."

"Gods perfect Love now does its perfect work here."

"I open myself up to All the Love Spirit Intends for me."

"I only draw to me Unconditional Love in my life, relationships and every experience."

Bring It Down to Earth! Utilize manifestation tools to bring into physical form all that is Divinely Intended from your Sacred-Heart!

Conscious living, always choosing to see as God Sees, and to be the Action of God, to be the Word of God, and the Love of God. 24/7 always choosing love, light, forgiveness and compassion.

I open myself to experience: Make the list, anything in your heart; anything you can imagine, all you have to do is open to receive and experience it. Your job is to tell God (your I Am Presence) what it is, and then sit back and receive it in its highest divinely intended form.

Treasure Map: make a vision board with an image of all of your desires. Put an Image of what God is for you and of the desired intent, and of you receiving it. Conclude with a statement of Gratitude. *"Thank you God Goddess, Spirit for bringing this or something greater into form for the highest good of all!"*

Conscious reminders, you can utilize amulets and talismans such as a string around your finger to give you a constant reminder to focus on love, light and joy.

Place all discordant experiences and emotions into the violet flame to clear the memory, record, cause, core and effect for all lifetimes. Claim what you want to experience or what is for your highest good. Now declare that this is the only thing you now draw towards you.

Transcend Duality, Be two people at once, the first person experiencing the humans experience through love compassion, forgiveness and acceptance. The send person choosing to create a new reality through activating the Divinely Intended Plan through conscious choice, affirmation and invocation.

Practice the act of the Immaculate Concept by holding a thought and space of purity or the divinely intended idea for an on behalf of others.

LIGHT ACTIVATION PLAY-SHEET

The Violet Ray is the 7th Ray of Freedom, Mastery, Transmutation and Daily Self-Care Routines and Rituals, for freeing the soul's records permanently and stepping off the wheel of karma.

Violet Flame Decree's (**7 MINUTES A DAY!**)... It is helpful to vocalize the violet flame decrees, each day, to dissolve negativity, fear, struggle, conflict and karmic debt.

"I AM A BEING OF VIOLET FIRE" "I AM THE PURITY GOD DESIRES".... Repeat......
I AM THE VIOLET FLAME IN ME BURNING OUT OF PURITY!

First invoke *divine protection*; I call forth Archangel Michael and his legions of blue light for divine protection and the ability to cut through all obstructions.

Invoke the Elohim of the Fourth Ray, Ascension Flame, Purity & Astrea. Surround oneself, house, space, building, community as examples with the white fire of Purity and the Blue Fire of Astrea. Envision two concentric circles of fire blazing light zig zaging around the waist or center. Envision the Blue Sword of Astrea piercing up through the center. This will snap off or de-magnify the miss-qualified parasitic entities bound to the molecular levels. This invocation may only provide 24 hour or short term freedom. Allowing one to utilize the Violet Flame for permanent freedom.

Next invoke the Violet Flame and guides of the Violet Ray, I call forth St. Germaine, Archangel Zadeickal, Holy Amethyst, Arcturias, Cosmic Victory and all Violet Ray Beings,

The violet flame fills my being; every molecule, particle and atom of my being is now filled with the violet flame. The violet flame fills me, moves through me and surrounds me. The violet flame fills and moves into my unconsciousness, sub-consciousness, consciousness, all my causal bodies and my aura. The violet flame moves into and fills my past, for this lifetime, all past life times and future lifetimes. The violet flame fills and surrounds my home, business and all of my life. The violet flame now fills and surrounds all of my family and our friends and loved ones.

The violet flame now fills and surrounds my town, the state, the country, and the Earth.

The violet flame now transmutes and frees me from all karmic debt.

Put all emotional, traumatic, less than, and karmic experiences into the violet flame, to TRANSMUTE and CLEAR THE MEMEORY, RECORD, CAUSE, CORE, and EFFECT, FOR ALL LIFETIMES, Give permission too, and thank the elemental beings, (builders of form) for releasing and letting go of all miss-qualified or miss-created forms and being brought forth into their current highest divinely intended purified form in the now.

Claim your divine birthright to experience; DIVINE FORGIVENESS, FREEDOM, LIBERTY, JUSTICE, OPPORTUNITIES & MERCY today and everyday. CLAIM VICTORY in this process!

With Mighty Victory I Am now Free and Liberated. I AM Light, I AM Love, I AM Free!! I AM ASCENDED...

Placing all suffering, pain, lack, judgment & dense experiences,

~Into the VIOLET FLAME!

Clearing the memory, record, cause, core & effect for all lifetimes!

(Storm dense emotions on this worksheet. Everything I hate, fear or judge. Everything that is unfair, unsafe, unjust, painful, harsh & difficult. All wrongs in the world & life. As you write and storm into this worksheet, each energy listed or acknowledged is automatically bathed in the purifying spiritual solvent of the VIOLET FLAME.)

I AM THE VIOLET FLAME IN ME BURNING OUT OF PURITY.....

(Sometimes it is helpful to burn this worksheet after stormed on
Take back your Divine Power to Create New Realities!)

Thank you SPIRIT for this or something better.

~FOR THE HIGHEST GOOD & JOY.. of ALL...

I Claim & Take Back My Divinely Intended Birthrights! I Claim and Take Back My Divinely Intended Power! I Choose & Take Back My Power to Choose! I NOW CHOOSE....

(Write out your highest dreams & desires from your sacred heart. Allow yourself to imagine & envision the unlimited. Be open to your superpowers with unlimited potentials. Release these to Spirit, without attachment to the outcome. Allow Spirit to bring them back to you in their highest form. Now accept them as Divine!)

If it is Divine Will, I AM open to Receive it; I AM open to BE it!

Choose Again! Now write out the highest desired life experiences.)

MASTER BEING WORKSHEET

INVOKE, DECREE, DECLARE, PROCLAIM, COMMAND, AFFIRM, INTEND, ENVISION, IMAGINE, RELEASE, RECIND, FORGIVE, UNDO, DELETE, CHOOSE AGAIN......

Three-Fold, Conscious Co-Creation Formula. Release, Invoke, Magnify.... Remember to SPEAK OUT LOUD, through the Power of the Spoken Word each sacred decree. Place your hand on your Sacred Heart with each decree. This automatically integrates the positive and negative polarities of duality, transcending third dimensional limitation into experiencing our Unlimited Multi-Dimensional Potential in Human Form.

1. I Now Release any agreement that:

2. Taking back my True Unlimited Divinely Intended Power of Source with-in me, I Now Choose to Co-Create:

I Claim I AM now _____, with Ease, Just for Being!

I Claim my Birthright to now experience, _____ with Ease, Just for Being!

I AM Open to experience _____, with Ease, Just for Being.

I ask this Sacred Request be Physically Demonstrated and Revealed though my own human knowing and understanding. I ask for the burning bush!

3. I Magnify this Sacred Intend by Choosing to only Draw this Intent to me and through Conscious Daily Reminders such as:

Thank you God, Mighty I AM Presence for the immediate manifestation of this, or something greater for the Highest Good of All.

LIGHT ACTIVATION PLAY-SHEET... EXAMPLE...
Putting Money into the Violet Flame

I thank all the Archangels, Ascended Masters, Elohim and Beings of Light for Divine and Angelic protection today & everyday. I call on Archangel Michael and his Legions of Blue Light to surround me with Golden Armor and Silver Light.

In the name of the beloved Mother Father God, The Alpha & Omega, I call to Ascended Master Saint Germaine, and All Violet Rayed Beings. I call my Higher-Self, my elemental White Fire Self. I thank God, the Elemental and Celestial Beings of Light to blaze the violet fire with the power and might of a thousand suns, the clear records or all money, exchange and monetary experiences through the Memory, Record, Cause, Core and effect for all lifetimes.

I NOW PLACE INTO THE VIOLET FLAME ALL MONEY, COMMERCE, POVERTY, LIMITATION, BROKENESS, LACK, MAKING DO, LIVING WITHOUT, SHAME, FEAR, GREED, HATRED, HORDING, OVERDRAFTS, LOAN DENIALS, CREDIT RECORDS, DEBT, GETTING BY, SURVIVING, MANIPULATION, ARGUMENTS, DISAGREEMENTS, EXCESSIVE FEES, ESCESSIVE CHARGES, EXCESSIVENESS, FILTH, LAUNDERING, GAMBELING, LOAN SHARKING, FUNNY MONEY, ILLIGITEMATE, BANKRUPSEY, CHARGE-OFFS, DOUBT, SKEPTISISM, UNFAIRNESS, INJUSTICE, BLAME, UNDU-RESPONSIBILIBTY, OBLIGATION, BURDENS, HARASSMENT, THIEVERY, FENCING, SLAVERY, ILNESS, FATIGUE, UNCERTIANNESS, EXCESSIVE TAXATION, UNFAIR TAXATION, UNJUST TAXATION, GUILT, STARVATION, ADDICTION, PIMPING, VANITY, IMPRISONMENT, ROTTING, MOLDING, EVIL INTENT, EVIL EYE, PERSECUTION, JUDGEMENT, GLUTTANY, GLOATING, BOASTING, VIOLENCE, BEATINGS, RUNNING, ESCAPISM, MISS-CREATING, MISS-QUALIFICATIONS, WASTE, MISERY, SUFFERING, CHANGE, CASH, GOLD, CREDIT, TABS, BILLS, UNEMPLOYMENT, INVOICES, ACCOUNTING SYSTEMS, BANKING SYSTEMS, LEAGAL SYSTEMS, CREDIT SYSTEMS, STOCKS, IRA'S BONDS, SAVINGS, CHECKS, RETIRMENTS FUNDS, MONETARY SYSTEMS, AND ANY OTHER AREA IN, AROUND, AND ABOUT MONEY, THROUGHOUT ALL TIME FROM EVERYWHERE, EVERYONE, AND EVERYTHING, TO NOW TRANSMUTE THE MEMORY, RECORD, CAUSE, CORE AND EFFECT.

THANK YOU, HIGHER-SELF, THANK YOU GOD I AM
For the full restoration of Divinely Intended Exchange.

(Create your own violet flame ceremony clearing the records of all miss-intended experiences, creations and less than desired experiences. Burn these as guided and then choose again by writing sown, claiming, speaking out-loud and visualizing the intended idea, blueprint or highest possibility.)

CHAPTER 4

---⬚---

EARTH=HEART

Healing the Sacred Heart. Restoring the Sacred Mind.

The Sacred Heart is the Ascension Chamber and Portal of Eternal Being.

Sacred Trust is restored and happens with ease when the Three-fold flame in the Sacred Heart is balanced and the wounds of the fall from divinity are healed through the One Unified Heart. Humanities collective history and the individual history of slavery, suffering, disease, lack, strife and separation have wounded the heart both individually and collectively. As the frequency of Mother Earth shifts, humans are also shifting. The old paradigm of hierarchical power ruling through fear, domination and no choice is being dissolved. Humans who embody the fullness of divinely intended power through the One Unified Heart are no longer controlled by the illusion of no power and no choice.

This evolutionary Paradigm Shift is the Unveiling of Divine Truth. The word, "Apocalypse" translated literally from Greek, is a disclosure of knowledge hidden from humanity in an era dominated by falsehood and misconception, i.e., a lifting of the veil or revelation," Wikipedia It is in the Unified Heart that each soul's divine guidance is revealed to them.

Being Heart Centered: The Heart Chakra is our Divine Center. It allows us to access all unconscious, past, future, and current wisdom we would like to know, simply by asking with intent. Traditionally the Heart Chakra has been assigned a lower and higher chamber. The Heart is where the multidimensional being unifies duality consciousness into the one truth or

124

one unified heart in the now. A simple way to be heart centered is to place your hand on your heart, while requesting information, setting intention or sending healing.

The three plumes of the heart are Love, Power, and Wisdom.

LOVE	(Pink) Receptive, or Having,	Left side of heart.
WISDOM	(Yellow) In the Now, or Being,	Center of heart.
POWER	(Blue) Action, or Doing,	Right side of heart.

Wisdom is always what balances and unites our dual nature/illusion.

It is through WISDOM that we are able to choose action verses inaction. Wisdom balances all power struggles and also the ego's desires. As we choose to align ourselves and actions with what is for the highest good, we put our higher self in the driver's seat, empowering us to unify love with wisdom and stepping into our divinity as creator beings.

It is through the Union of the Sacred Feminine and the Sacred Masculine selves that we enter into the Sacred Marriage of our Higher Selves. This is an essential process to move from the third dimensional world of duality/limitation, into the fifth dimensional world of unlimited potential as creator beings. As creator beings it is our purpose to create heaven on Earth, by being Spirit incarnate in physical form. This is the Sacred Trust!

Open Hearted: Radiant Light is our Divine Nature. We can ask Higher-Self how many layers of armor are layered over our sacred heart. These layers are in the causal body, or record body... We can ask what materials the armor is and how this material has served the soul during incarnation for protection. Then we can ask our higher-self to remove all records of heart armor in a divinely ordered and nourishing easy way. It is important to Invoke and Declare our intent to have an open heart of Radiant Light.

Affirmation: **Place Hand on Heart and speak out loud, through the power of the spoken word.**

"I AM ready to live Open Heartedly. I ask my Higher Self, to remove all heart armor from my Sacred Heart in an easy comfortable way. I Claim my Birthright to live Open Heartedly, My Sacred Heart is a Fiery Vortex of Light. The Sacred Fire is restored in my Sacred Heart and lit is the center of every atom of my Being."

LIBERATION IN LIGHT: Throughout history many humans have had to hide or withdraw to be safe, especially in childhood. Any form of withdrawal and contraction of the Intended self creates an energetic withdrawal of ones Intended Energy, Divine Knowing and Intended Guidance. These create hiding contracts. Some souls have had a mission to be a wisdom keeper and had to make a contract of secrecy to hide wisdom such as in mystery schools to keep the wisdom safe. Many lifetimes in history people of knowledge were persecuted, tortured and killed. These souls then vowed to keep wisdom hidden. So now they are often lost energetically and need to take back their power to know, have and reveal truth and wisdom freely easily and safely.

Affirmation: **Place Hand on Heart and speak out loud, through the power of the spoken word.**

"I Stand in my Light, Follow Truth from my Heart and Hold up my Torch. My Torch Burns through all Obstacles and Lights my Divinely Intended Pathway! ALL IS REVEALED IN THE LIGHT TODAY! ALL IS LIBERATED IN LIGHT TODAY!" Lady Liberty

FREE WILL, CONSCIOUS CHOICE, FREEDOM. To choose is to will.

Each human has free will and the right to choose 24-7 all their own actions, thoughts, beliefs and experiences. If a choice is not aligned with the Higher-Self then it is not co-creating heaven on earth, and will bind one-self to the karmic equivalents. Each choice and action aligned with the Highest Good of our Individualized Sacred Heart does co-create Heaven on Earth and begins to restore the Sacred Trust.

Affirmation: **Place Hand on Heart and speak out loud, through the power of the spoken word.**

> *"I Claim Free Will as my Divine Birthright! I take Back my Divine Unlimited Power to Choose Again. I Now choose to Create _____. I send this Free-Will back to myself throughout all time, space and dimensions. I Ask the Angels and Elemental Beings to do this for me."*

> *"I take back my Divine Power to Stand! I Stand in my Light. I Stand in Divine Truth. I Stand for Love. I Stand for Truth. I Stand for God. It is safe to Stand in my light, and truth."*

BALANCING THE THREE-FOLD FLAME

Love-Wisdom-Power

POWER: The flame of Power is Blue and has the quality of Action.

The flame of power is on the right side of the body. It carries the positive polarity of the Sacred Masculine. It Corresponds to Air, Fire, Beliefs, Values, Spirit. The Inner Warrior, and the mental causal body. **The Divine Plan is co-created through the sacred intent and action of the Inner Masculine.**

Power has the action energy or doing energy. This energy steps up to take action by, providing, protecting and supporting us. In its divinity this energy waits to know what is in the heart, and then takes action to support manifest and obtain this sacred desire of our highest intended good.

As humans our society has often taught us that the mind should rule the emotions. The emotional qualities of the feminine will get one into trouble, while the masculine mind qualities will keep one safe. This is a human judgment and is a wound that must be healed for us to be our higher selves on earth. Anytime something is judged it separates it from its divinity, thereby limiting it. As humans release all judgment of each other and of ourselves, we can be empowered to step into our creative potential. By stating what we would like to experience verses what we are experiencing, we send forth our creative force, the spoken word. It is through this power that we can create or destroy.

ACTIVATE DIVINE POWER.

Place your hand on your Sacred Heart and Speak Out loud, through the Power of the Spoken Word.

> *"Divine Power is activated in me. I take back my divine birthright and power to be free, and to create new realities. I claim my divine birthright to experience eternal peace."*

> *"I now align myself with the Higher Will of God. Gods will not my own works in and through me, everyone, and everything. Aligning ones will with the higher will of Spirit is the most important thing you can do to become ones highest self on earth!"*

To Free up the Blue Flame, from your own and mankind's collective judgment, that the male energy is harsh, inflexible and unyielding.

> *"The forgiving father is made alive in me, everyone and everything. The allowing and accepting father is now made alive in me, everyone and everything. The Sacred masculine now resides in me, in everyone, and in everything. Begin today to actively love, forgive and act with compassion and kindness towards yourself, and everyone."*

Wound to Heal is: Force is power verses Infinite Source within me is power. Also all Judgment of power Judgment of anything including self creates more of what the judgment is.

Birthright is to Take back all the Divinely Intended Powers to Co-Create Joyful Safe Life as an Unlimited Being. God, Goddess, Master in Human Form. Choice =Will, Too choose is to will.

Affirmation: **Place Hand on Heart and speak out loud, through the power of the spoken word.**

"I Claim my Divine Birthright and open myself to experience all the Divine Power of God Source in my Sacred Heart intended for me. I Claim Free-Will as my Birthright. I Claim my Birthright to Choose. I Choose for my Divine Good. I Claim Freedom as my Divine Birthright. I Claim my Divine Unlimited Potential to give birth to new form freely, and easily. I Claim my Birthright to say NO, I Say no to all obstacles, blockages, density or anything that would keep me from my Divinely Intended Good. I Claim my Birthright to be Inherently Safe and Protected, just for being. I Claim Eternal Peace as my Divine Birthright. Peace with my past, present and future. I AM at the Center of Eternal Peace."

Love: The Flame of Love is pink and has the quality of Receptivity.

The flame of Love is on the left side of the body. It is receptive and having. It carries the negative polarity of the Divine Feminine. It corresponds to water, earth, body, flesh, matter, the inner child and the emotional causal body. **The Divine Plan is received intuitively and sensed or known through the Inner Feminine.**

This is the flame that allows us to receive. All our intuition comes through our receptive qualities. It's also the having energy. It's allows us to receive inspiration, understanding, love, acceptance, money, acknowledgment, everything that we need to have for our existence in physical life. This heart flame can be likened to the holy receptacle receiving Divine Love. When we sacrifice what is in our hearts, we sacrifice our ability to receive Spirits rich substance into our lives.

As humans our society has often taught us that the feminine qualities of emotion are less than the male qualities of reason. That to be selfish is a sin, and that it is admirable to be of spirit and not of the body. These beliefs in essence sacrifice the feminine, receptive flame. In reality we are perfect divine beings of light, accepted by spirit as sacred and perfect, worthy of divine love. As infinite beings of unlimited potential, when we allow ourselves to receive the yearnings of our heart, we open ourselves to receive all the riches and love that Spirit is already offering us. When we say yes to what is in our heart, Spirit says yes to us and sends it forth into physical reality. The more we allow ourselves to receive what is in our heart, the more we have and can give to our family, friends and loved ones. This is how we become instruments of Spirit, channels for infinite love, light and prosperity.

ACTIVATE DIVINE LOVE,

Place your hand on your Sacred Heart and Speak Out loud, through the Power of the Spoken Word.

> *"Divine Love is now activated in me. Divine Love is activated in everyone, everywhere and everything. Divine Love now does its perfect work in me, everyone and everything. I claim my divine birthright to experience infinite abundance".*

> *"The empowered nourishing mother in her divinely intended form, is now activated in me, everyone and everything. Allow yourself to bring the divine feminine back into her rightful space, as a sacred being sitting beside the male in perfect balance. This needs to be done for each individual as well as the universal collective."*

Wound to Heal is: Sacrifice of self for others, being the burden bearer, the wounded healer and taking responsibility for others, especially their emotional experiences.

Birthright is to experience an Infinite Supply of LOVE and all physical, emotional, mental, and spiritual needs.

Affirmation: **Place Hand on Heart and speak out loud, through the power of the spoken word.**

> *"I Claim the Highest, Divinely Intended, Eternal, Unconditional Love as my Divine Birthright. I Claim my Being is Inherently Loved, and Worthy just for Being. I open myself to experience an Infinite Supply of Love, Acceptance, Nourishment, Finances, Provisions, and everything that God intends to support my Highest Good. There is Enough! It is Safe to say yes to me and to what is in my sacred heart. I open myself to experience even greater levels of self-love every day.*

It is safe to feel good. Love is Safe. I AM now Divinely Nourished by everywhere, everyone, and everything. Only Unconditional Love resides in my life today and every day. I Love all people and all people love me, without attachment. Unconditional Love is the only reality I choose to attract in my life. I am now loved by everyone, with ease, just for being. I now experience Unconditional Divine Love in everyone, everywhere and everything. ONLY LOVE IS REAL!"

WISDOM, The Flame of Wisdom is Yellow and has the quality of Being.

The wisdom flame is the center of the body. Wisdom or Being is in the NOW. It has the qualities of Knowing, Seeing, Hearing, and Being as God Goddess or Angel in Human Form. It is the Higher-Self, I Am Presence and the experience of the Fullness of Life! **The Divine Plan is Understood, Realized and Actualized through the inner Divine Guidance of Crystalline Christ Consciousness.**

Wisdom is the union of love and understanding. It is here that the union of the sacred feminine and masculine merges into our Higher Self. Through the wisdom of our higher self we invite the qualities of divine understanding and clarity into our lives. This is the energy of living in the now fully through bliss and joy.

The wound carried on the yellow ray is the wound of suffering. Any belief or contract that being in the body is painful, being in relationship is painful or that life is pain, will create suffering in our lives. Any vows of suffering or poverty will wound the flame of wisdom. As creator beings we have chosen to incarnate into physical form to create heaven on earth. In the fifth dimension we are integrating the maximum amount of light and spirit into our bodies, and into the earth. Any belief that the body limits us is a judgment separating us from our higher selves and must be healed. As creator beings we must gain mastery through the physical body, as much as the emotional, mental, and soul bodies.

ACTIVATE THE WISDOM FLAME,

Place your hand on your Sacred Heart and Speak Out loud, through the Power of the Spoken Word.

> *"I activate divine wisdom within me. Divine understanding is activated in me, everyone and everything! I claim my divine birthright to know as God knows."*

> *"I now bring into my conscious awareness any energetic (conscious, or unconscious) that is no longer for my highest good. These are now CLEARLY being revealed to me through DIVINE UNDERSTANDING. This process happens with ease, and in a divinely ordered way."*

Wound to Heal is: Suffering, being in body, relationship, or on earth is painful.

Birthright is to experience Sacred Union in Joyful Fulfilling Life with ease, JUST FOR BEING! It is our opportunity to CHOOSE through this Divine Wisdom a new reality and begin to Co-Create Heaven on Earth through the Power of the Spoken Word.

Affirmation: Place Hand on Heart and speak out loud, through the power of the spoken word.

> *"Divine Understanding is now activated in me and my life. I take back my birthright to know as God, Goddess and Spirit Knows, through my own heart, my own knowing and personal understanding. I Claim Joyful Life as my Divine Birthright. I Claim Easy as my Birthright. I only draw to me life and relationships that are easy and joyful. I take back my power and Birthright to Embrace the Fullness of Life. I AM fully embraced by Life. I AM fully embraced by God. I AM fully embraced by Love. I Claim Safe Sacred Touch as my Birthright. I AM touched by Love. I AM touched by God. I AM touched by everything good. I AM fulfilled by Love. I have the Power to Love. I have the Power to Forgive. I have the power to Choose*

Again. Only Divine Order now resides in my mind, in my body and in my life. Only Divine Order now resides in all timing. I walk in perfect timing with the Universe."

HEALING THE SACRED HEART

Balancing the Flames, Restoring the Sacred Fire.

The repeated outplay of Miasmic Distortions is called Karma.

The Law of Karma states "whatever we measure out to ourselves or others is measured back to us."

When humans experience trauma, or life in a way which that does not match our divinity or spiritual truth, our souls will often assess this situation as not being what we know as spiritual truth, we then take action into a pattern that serves to protect ourselves. The problem is that these patterns while serving us in the third dimension, no longer serve us in a fifth dimensional world as creator beings. These patterns are called contracts, agreements or vows. They are made from a place of being separate from our divinity and they limit or bind us in the lower vibrations of duality and illusion. These contacts are the wounds that keep us from moving into our unlimited potential. Soul level contracts become karmic attachment's that our soul is bound too, until a new soul choice is made. As humans we store and carry these limiting contracts and karmic bindings in the shadow and unconscious awareness of our being. This includes the cellular memory, the RNA and the DNA. The soul's enteric template may be referred to as the akashic records.

> **Miasims:** The distortions, mutations and all lower vibration (dense) disharmonic thought forms from past moments are known as miasms. Miasms distort the flow of energy and identity through the human system. Each lifetime's miasms are compounded, creating repetitive patterns in the current lifetime. Miasms are responsible for the manifestations of disease and disharmonic conditions within the body and life structure. Each person's miasmic imprint establishes their design and function of DNA.

Transmuting miasms with the process of embodying higher identity levels allows activation of higher DNA strands. The activation of higher strands initiates a realignment in a person's life direction and physical health towards a more harmonious and joyful path. http://www.selftransform.net/DNA.htm

According to the book Gem Elixirs and Vibrational healing, Volume 2, by Gurudas, there are 4 types of misaims.

1. Planetary Misaims are stored in the collective consciousness of the planet and in the ethers. They penetrate into the physical body, but are not stored in the physical body.

2. Inherited Misaims are stored in the cellular memories. (4 types of inherited misaims are the Psora, Syphilitic, Sycotic, and Tuberculosis)

3. Acquired Misaims are acute diseases, infections or petrochemical toxicities acquired during a given lifetime.

4. Steller Misaims are distortions of separation as the cosmic level.

After an acute state of illness, these acquired miasmatic traits settle into the subtle bodies and the molecular and cellular levels where they manifest as problems in energetic and physical forms or manifestations of illness, pain and suffering.

RELEASING CONTRACTS, & CREATING NEW REALITIES

Somatic's, Our physical body holds the space of miasisms, energetic contracts, vows, agreements, judgments and karmic attachment's or bindings. Soul level contracts or vows are held in the cellular memory, DNA, and in the etheric templates called the causal bodies. These are the soul records called the Akash. Humans are multidimensional Beings, having multiple sensory experiences at one time. These experiences are in multiple dimensions at once. Some are conscious and some unconscious. These records or frequencies are bound somatically, and they are the energetics that manifest in physical form causing discord, strife, disease and fear based consciousness.

The Wheel of Karma is a repetitive pattern of duality and separation that may be held for many life times. Sometimes it is genetically bound and repeated through ancestral bloodlines. Continuation of these polarized patterns of energetics held in the etheric templates or causal bodies will continue to manifest in physical form lowering the souls vibrational frequencies in a process called *devolution or separation.*

Balancing Polarity and Transcending Duality Heart

As Planet Earth raises in vibrational frequency, the outdated 3rd dimensional paradigm of separation, duality, judgment, domination, control, lack and suffering no longer serve the Human Being (Hue-Man = Rainbow-Being). Humans must be Resonant with Earth. As the frequency of each being incarnated on Earth are One Collective Consciousness. One Heart.

These unconscious energetics, agreements and contracts were made while living in a third dimensional earth. We are now living in a time of the intended blue-print, a fifth dimensional world. The old, outdated energetics held in our being are dense creating obstacles.

Polarity: Electric, Magnetic

To be creator beings living in a fifth dimensional world, we need to upgrade our matrix from one of disempowerment to one of being divinely empowered. This is done by releasing any old dense energetic contracts, agreements, memories, stuffed emotions and limiting self-governing structures. All old outdated energetics are in fact a **magnet** and draw to us what they are. Remember we have the power to create or transmute through the science of the spoken word! Invocation and decree through the activated Sacred Heart Torus or electromagnetic sphere is **electric activation of the intended plan.** Balancing the polarity, transcending duality and co-creating the new divinely intended life of freedom, joy and bliss. Humans need to be equally magnetic and electric to transcend limitation.

Place your hand on your Sacred Heart and Speak Out loud, through the Power of the Spoken Word.

"I release any soul level contract, vow, agreement, or pact that I have ever made...And that is stored in the cellular memory or any part of myself, conscious or unconscious being that...................(fill in the blank). I am now FREE to CREATE NEW REALITIES!! I choose to create...(choose the highest intended idea). I only draw towards me, people, situations, or events that are of love, safe, trustworthy and of divine order."" *"Anything not of these is now banished from my life!!! Only divine Order exists in my Mind, Body, and Life! I AM CONNECTED!! I DO BELONG!!"*

Conscious Language is the Master Key for healing.

Crystalline Consciousness is choosing to live through deliberate conscious intent, 24 hours a day and 7 days a week. Choosing thought forms that are aligned with the One Unified Good and Divine Blueprint Upgraded in the Now.

Becoming aware of the Virtues of 12 cosmic rays of the solar hierarchy allows the individual to become conscious of the dormant virtues held within the center of every molecule in humans. Allowing the individual to activate each virtue or sacred aspect of intended life in those places and people it is not experienced.

Choosing Conscious language, through setting Sacred Intent, Affirming and Activating in the outer experience of relationship's and life, both programs and heals the DNA and Miasmic distortions. Resulting in Restoration of Health, Freedom and Soul Liberation. This is the purification and clearing of the souls akashic/karmic records at the individual and collective levels.

By Utilizing the science of the spoken word we can activate the Wisdom Flame and Divine Understanding in ourselves and in others. To wake up the wisdom flame, invoke Divine Understanding, and Clarity. We can invoke Divine Understanding and Clarity now be made alive in oneself, everyone and everything. As we activate the wisdom flame, we are able to become aware of how we have layered each of our sacred heart flames with the veils of illusion that keep us stuck in a third dimensional world of denseness.

> *"I Thank Spirit for the Activation of Divine Understanding in the Hearts and Mind of all Beings for the Restoral of Heaven on Earth today."*

Divine Protection. It is intended to be safe in the process of becoming empowered, fulfilled and whole. The human's ability to co-create is the Divinely Intended Plan. Humans co-create hand in hand with the Spiritual Realms through the octaves of Light. Remember the spiritual realms are not separate from us as **All Are One** in the higher dimensions of light. Rather the spiritual realms are the individuated aspects of Divine Intelligence. The human's power is in part to know the omnipresence of being eternal through the aligned and balanced sacred heart. The human is unlimited as an eternal soul. The Human vessel is the Sacred Temple allowing the process of God Manifestation to take place.

The first ray of God is the Ray of Gods Will, Power Purpose and Protection. When these qualities are experienced in an individual's life, they will be at PEACE. Eternal Peace and the ability to experience peace is the intended right of the first ray. It is intended that human have the Inherent Power to co-create Heaven On Earth through the Power of God, Christ Consciousness in the sacred heart, through free-will, power, purpose and protection.

In fear based consciousness the human becomes disempowered and their vibrational frequency is lowered. If ignored or pushed away the fear will be stuffed into the unconscious cellular level and be food for the archonic entities. Fear is common and normal for individuals to experience. Fear is the emotion that alerts the human to safety. As fear and struggle arise in the human experience the individual is able to invoke the guides of the first ray for assistance and support in the multi-dimensional realms of human being. The Archangels of the first ray are Michael and Faith.

I call forth my Higher-Self. I call forth Archangel Michael and his legions of blue light for divine protection and the ability to cut through all obstructions. I thank my Higher-Self and Archangel Michael for removing the fear and all entities. I thank Archangel Michael for cutting all unwanted psychic chords, attachments or energetic agreements that are not aligned with Divine Will as my free liberated ascended self in the now.

As each negative emotion comes to the awareness, invite it into love and ask the angels to escort it into love. Every emotion that is recognized and acknowledged and invited into love will begin to transform into its higher less intensive forms. Transmuting and lifting the heaviness felt by the individual. Freeing the cellular memories and clearing the way for the light body to be activated.

I invite all my fear or negative emotions out of my emotional body and into love. I thank my higher-self and angels for doing this for me.

Identify each emotion and repeat as they arise. Over time the fear will subside and be replaced with courage and strength. Each emotion serves the human equally as each thought. Both the thoughts of the mental body and the emotions of the emotional body are in service to the Higher-Self, which is now activated and resides in the Sacred-Heart.

As the individual begins to take back their divinely intended power to be safe, at peace and co-create in accompaniment with Divine Will they are propelled into the Sacred White Fire of Purity. The fourth ray of God is the ray of ascension it is considered to be the Mother Flame (Shakti) that is activated at the base of the spine to raise the kundalini or sacred white fire as a purifying force for light body activation. The fourth ray lesson is to co-create harmony in the experience of conflict. Out of chaos comes order. The Elohim of the fourth ray in matter (the human body) are activators of the sacred fire that burn off the dross of density of human karma or the unconscious energetics stored with in the cellular memories and records called the Akash. In eastern philosophy the fourth ray is Kali-Ma the Goddess of Transmutation.

I Invoke Elohim of the Fourth Ray, the Ascension Flame, Pui Astrea. I Surround myself, with the White Fire of Purity and the Blue Fire of Astrea. I envision the Blue Sword of Astrea cutting up through the center aligned with my spine. I now surround my home and work and relationships with the blue and white flame of Purity and Astrea and slide blue sword up through the center to cut away all anti-love energetics.

Envision two concentric circles of fire blazing light zig zagging around the waist or center. Envision the Blue Sword of Astrea piercing up through the center. This will snap off or de-magnify the miss-qualified parasitic entities bound to the molecular levels. This invocation may only provide 24 hour or short term freedom. Allowing one to utilize the Violet Flame for permanent freedom.

This invocation is helpful for people who experience anxiety or are very empathic. Especially when entering into a public crowd. By invoking purity and astrea through the two concentric circles of light and blue sword, one can enter into a crowded space and not pick up other people's attachments, implants or similar unconscious energetics that would have attached to the person without doing this process.

TRANSMUTATION with the Violet Flame,

The Violet Ray is the Seventh Ray. The Violet Ray is the seventh ray of Self-Mastery, Transmutation, and Purification. The Violet Flame is A Perfect Combination of the pink, and blue of the Sacred Heart flames. The violet flame is what balances the feminine and masculine polarities of duality. The Violet Flame is a powerful way to transmute any energetics that keep us bound in the illusion of duality. The violet flame is a spiritual solvent that frees us from past karmic debt and helps us to restore wholeness to the body and achieve spiritual union with the higher self. Invoking the violet flame through violet flame decrees for 7 to 11 minutes a day, will begin to free up and release dense energies and karmic debt, in one's past and present. This one continuous activity is the most powerful and important ritual that anyone can do to clear karmic debt, experiences and lift the experience or restriction or oppression.

Repetitive Chant's: *"I am a being of violet Fire; I am the purity God Desires".* Repeat...

"I Am the Violet Flame in me burning out of Purity". Repeat...

Affirmation: Place Hand on Heart and speak out loud, through the power of the spoken word.

"I place into the violet flame (quality/experience, such as fear, pain, suffering, obstacles) _____ to clear and erase the memory, record, cause core, and effect for all lifetimes.

Through the Power of the ONE Heart and Crystalline Christ Consciousness in me, I Claim my Sacred Dominion and Choose to co-create a New Reality.

I Now Choose to create_____.
I thank my Higher-Self and Angels for doing this work for me.

I Command and give permission to the Elementals (who are binding the energetic, records in place) To now be Freed, Released, Let Go and Undone. I give you permission to shift form and shape, into the Divinely Intended Free Form in the Now. (as the divine plan intends this experience to be).

Give permission too, and thank the elemental beings, (builders of form) for releasing and letting go of all miss-qualified or miss-created forms and being brought forth into their current highest divinely intended purified form in the now.

Healing the Power Flame of Sacred Heart th
DIVINE RELEASE!!

PLUME OF POWER: *Healing Wounds with the Sacred Masculine. Doing, Action, Air, Fire, Beliefs, Values, Spirit. The Inner Warrior, or Intellectual body.*

Wound to Heal is: Force is power verses Infinite Source within me is power. The soul must release all Judgment of Power. Judgment is a curse. What is measured out to ourselves or others is measured back to us. Judgment of anything including self creates and manifests in physical form, more of what this judgment is.

Birthright is to take back all the Divinely Intended Powers to Co-Create Joyful Safe Life as an Unlimited Being. God, Goddess, Master in Human Form. Choice =Will, Too choose is to will.

PLACE HAND ON SACRED HEART AND SPEAK OUT LOUD, WITH THE POWER OF THE SPOKEN WORD!

I Release and Rescind all agreements that power is the use of Force and I have no choice but to accept the Force of others or I have no choice but to use Force to protect myself, family or others.

I Release and Rescind all agreements that I am unsafe.

I Release and Rescind all judgment and condemnation of power and those who have abused power or who are in authority or power for all lifetimes, human and non-human.

I Release and Rescind all judgment of Power, and in those people or structures or systems of power or authority.

I Release and Rescind all agreements that I must do something, perform, be perfect, try harder, do more, compete, win, prove myself, be tougher, be larger, be in a role, have control, be only logical or rational, force the matter, harden myself, control the situation.

I Release and Rescind all agreements that I have NO CHOICE but to be a victim, suffer, be in pain, be smaller, shrink, withdraw, hide, give-up, be less than, be quiet, to not know, and not understand.

I Release and Rescind all agreements that I must hide to be safe.

I Release and Rescind all agreements that I do not matter, life does not matter, love does not matter, my dreams and purpose does not matter, God does not matter.

I Release and Rescind all agreements I have to wait, I am incomplete, it will never happen, I will always....I release always, only, forever, never, what is done is done, you can never go back, I am condemned, I am a sinner, I am unworthy or I am eternally dammed.

I Release and Rescind all agreements that life or my life is a waste, has no purpose, meaning or value.

I Release and Rescind all agreements that I should suffer eternally, and deserve to be punished and suffer.

I Release and Rescind all agreements to Never Have Power, my True Divinely Intended Power.

I Release and Rescind all agreements that to Love or Forgive is a weakness.

I Release and Rescind all agreements that God is a punishing or jealous God.

ADD TO THE LIST: I Release and Rescind.....

I Release and Rescind all agreements that:

Placing each of the above experiences into the VIOLET FLAME, to CLEAR the memory, record, cause, core and effect for all incarnations! I thank the Angels for doing this for me. Choosing to Love Now!

Taking Back my Divinely Intended Power to be a Co-Crea
I NOW choose to create that my Divinely Intended Power
in my Sacred-Heart is manifesting as:

> *List out desired intentions as God intends or the Divine Blueprint or Unlimited Possibility:*

Healing the Love Flame of Sacred Heart through DIVINE RELEASE!!

PLUME OF LOVE: *Healing the wounds with the Divine Feminine. Receptive, Having. Water, Earth, Matter and Elemental Body. The Inner Child or Emotional Body.*

> ***Wound to Heal is:*** Sacrifice of self for others, being the burden bearer, the wounded healer. Taking responsibility for others, especially their emotional experiences.
>
> Birthright is to experience an Infinite Supply of LOVE and all physical, emotional, mental, and spiritual needs.

PLACE HAND ON SACRED HEART AND SPEAK OUT LOUD, WITH THE POWER OF THE SPOKEN WORD!

I Release and Rescind all agreements that Love is Conditional.

I Release and Rescind all agreements that Love is painful.

I Release and Rescind all agreements that Love is hatred.

I Release and Rescind all agreements that Love is sacrifice.

I Release and Rescind all agreements that is unsafe to love or be loved.

I Release and Rescind all agreements that it is my job, duty, responsibility, or sacrifice to love others.

143

I Release and Rescind all agreements that it is my duty, job or responsibility to fixit or others.

I Release and Rescind all agreements that any other persons love, wellbeing, feelings, or emotions are my responsibility.

I Release and Rescind all agreements that It is my purpose to love those who only hate or are angry.

I Release all agreements that there Not Enough, life, love, nourishment, money, or anything that serves my highest good.

I Release and Rescind all agreements that love is blind.

I Release and Rescind all agreements that women are less than men.

I Release and Rescind all agreements that to be emotional or have emotions is weak.

I Release all agreements of separation.

I Release and Rescind all agreements that I don't fit in, I don't belong, I am different, I am separate, I am unworthy, I am ugly or I am anything less than the Divinely Intended.

I Release and Rescind all agreements that God is a Man or that women is less than a man.

ADD TO THE LIST: I Release and Rescind.

I Release and Rescind all agreements that:

Placing each of the above experiences into the VIOLET FLAME, to CLEAR the memory, record, cause, core and effect for all incarnations! I thank the Angels for doing this for me. Choosing to Love Now!

Taking Back my Divinely Intended Power to be a Co-Crea
Being I NOW choose to create that my Divinely Intended Love is
manifesting as:

List our desired intentions as God intends or the Divine Blueprint or
Unlimited Possibility:

Healing the Wisdom Flame of Sacred Heart through DIVINE RELEASE!!

PLUME OF WISDOM: *Higher-Self, I Am Presence. Being in the NOW,*
The Fullness of Life!

> ***Wound to Heal is:*** Suffering, being in body, relationship, or on
> earth is painful.

> Birthright is to experience Sacred Union in Joyful Fulfilling Life
> with ease, JUST FOR BEING! It is our opportunity to CHOOSE
> through this Divine Wisdom a new reality and begin to Co-Create
> Heaven on Hearth through the Power of the Spoken Word.

PLACE HAND ON SACRED HEART AND SPEAK OUT LOUD,
WITH THE POWER OF THE SPOKEN WORD!

I Release and Rescind all judgment and condemnation of Humanity.

I Release and Rescind all judgment and condemnation of Love.

I Release and Rescind all judgment and condemnation of Power.

I Release and Rescind all judgment and condemnation of Life.

I Release all judgment and condemnation of myself through this life and all
lifetimes.

I Release and Rescind all judgment of my past, my present and my future.

...dgment of Humanity's past, present, and future.

...scind all judgment of the government, corporations, business, ...nocrats, politics' the legal system, the educational system, the medical system, healthcare, insurance agencies and all structures, systems, the illuminati, secret societies, Genetically Modified Organisms, Monsanto, everyone, everywhere, and everything.

I Release and Rescind all agreements that being human, or living on Earth is painful.

I Release and Rescind all agreements that life is hardship, suffering, or pain.

I Release and Rescind all agreements that being in relationship is painful or hard.

I Release and Rescind all agreements that life is a dog eat dog world.

I Release and Rescind all agreements that humans are destroying earth.

I Release and Rescind all agreements that I must wait for my good.

I Release and Rescind all agreements that there is no time or I must hurry.

I Release and Rescind all agreements that I don't matter, love does not matter or life does not matter.

ADD TO THE LIST: I Release and Rescind.

I Release and Rescind all agreements that:

Placing each of the above experiences into the VIOLET FLAME, to CLEAR the memory, record, cause, core and effect for all incarnations! I thank the Angels for doing this for me. Choosing to Love Now!

Taking Back my Divinely Intended Power to be a Co-Creator Being I NOW choose to create that my Divinely Intended Wisdom and Divine Understanding is manifesting as:

List our desired intentions as God intends or the Divine Blueprint or Unlimited Possibility:

RESTORING THE SACRED MIND: (the sacred mind is the descending triangle, the sacred heart is the ascending triangle, they merge in the Sacred Heart, to become diamond consciousness and then activate the Torsion Field, Star Merkaba, Star of David, or Solar Light Body.)

DIVINE INTELLIGENCE, called cognition. *"Cognition is the process by which the sensory input is transformed, reduced, elaborated, stored, recovered, and used. Cognition is a faculty for the processing of information, applying knowledge, and changing preferences. Cognition, or cognitive processes, can be natural or artificial, conscious or unconscious."* Wikipedia.

Divine Mind is Buddha Consciousness. Divine Intelligence and Understanding as an Eternal Being in temporary human form. It is choosing to live through deliberate conscious intent 24/7 as co-creator in accompaniment with Source through the octaves of light. Tapping into the unlimited potential through conscious choice, and activation of this sacred intent through the Power of the Spoken Word, Sound, Toning, Mantra, Frequency, Action, Rhythm, Constancy and Choice. Through full activation of this Buddha consciousness the individual experiences "Samadhi" a Sanskrit term meaning absolute bliss and euphoria. When the individual reaches higher states of enlightenment or frequency the being begins to loose sense of self or individuation. Bliss is experienced as a heightened state of ecstasy in extreme experiences the being may lose a sense of self and urges for food or other physical desires.

The Book Autobiography of a Yogi is recommended reading for understanding these types of phenomena. Some yogis and individuals begin to live without food or water taking in the energy of the sun and internalized activated light as sole source of nourishment.

The Fifth Ray of Spirit is the ray of concrete and abstract knowledge. In other words It is both the lower human mind and the higher or sacred human mind. In the veils of illusion, the individual may experienc having no choice or being controlled by an external force. The human mind may be filled with the thought forms and programs of other people's cognitions, beliefs or of false inorganic programs implanted or overlaid on the individual from the archonic entities.

Many adult humans are storing or holding the thought forms of their parents, ancestors, and culture or family members. When the individual is obligated to another person or group through a soul level contract or agreement, the individual is then open to carry that group karmic energy. Or the individual's obligation will allow similar or like energy to join in band together and expand in size. As an example if a child feels responsible for their mother and chooses to be good or quiet to help her. As an adult this person may be open, store, carry or be obligated to similar women's energy, or to all mothers' energies, or to all women they might know.

In the etheric dimensions of the records there is no separation. So any agreement or contract with mom becomes all women. And any contract or agreement with father becomes all men. At a societal level, the mother or feminine energy is the substance of society. The father or masculine energy is the rules, structure and order of society. Money is feminine and the banking rules are masculine.

Unlimited Potential with Infinite Possibilities. Divine Mind

> *"I AM the mind of God. I AM the thought of God. I think as God Goddess thinks."*

The Divine Mind is the sacred mind of the individuated God Goddess in human form. Each human is in the process of updating their **"Self-Governing Structures"** or cognitions. Their perceptions and the way they think about self about others and about life. ALL WAYS, MEANS AND MEASURES are being renewed and restored to the Highest Intended Upgraded ways, means and measures in the now as divinely intended.

In this Paradigm Shift, I say New Day, New Way. Meaning : being updated in the now.

There is a way, I open myself to know the way, have the way ana ve ine way.

The root word "way" comes from the meaning or a safe passage, road, or water-way. The Way is the Divinely Intended Path for the soul to fulfill its Divine Plan. Life is intended to be easy and flow through Divine Understanding activated in the sacred heart. Life is easy when the Sacred Mind and Sacred Heart are aligned with the conscious choice and actions of the co-creator god goddess in human form. When life becomes difficult or challenging the individual may be willing or pushing for something that is not aligned with the divine good of self.

May Divine Will be activated, aligned and reside in me, my mind and my life, with ease just for being.

This means anyway one has measured their own success or the success of others is ready to be shifted into the empowered cognitions or thought forms of being. If each individual is worthy, sacred and divine then the individual can Honor the divine in self and honor the divine in others, Known as the term, Namaste.

Because each thought creates what it is in form. Fighting to win, creates more fighting. I must admit that I dislike the term spiritual warrior. I prefer the term Spiritual Activator of Truth. Justice, Peace, Light and Love. However if the energy is not charged in the individual it is not karmic. Judgment of others often accompanies the individuals desire to be perfect so they win or achieve the goal. Self-Righteousness is a polarized experience of trying to measure up by being the best perceived for measuring up or winning.

There are no measurements in life. Ascension is not a goal it is a process of becoming light. Having to do something to gain access to heaven or to prove oneself worthy is a soul wound. So is, performing to fit in or be safe. Having to measure up or win. The warrior wound with honor is the contract or agreement that one has to fight to win, fight to live, or die with a sword in the hand to enter into Valhalla, heaven or be honorable in that society of culture. **In the new paradigm Honor is and can be experienced as Eternal Peace. It can be honorable to die and live in peace.**

The Means. Having to pay for one's good, or perform for one's good or sacrifice for one's good are also being updated. Debt Slavery is a limiting experience created by controllers to keep humans enslaved through burden, work, suffering and lack. Any means by which one has known as the way to be safe or fulfill ones plan is ow being upgraded into the New Paradigm, where everything in the universe is conspiring to support and provide for self. As the individuals invokes the desire, Higher-Self evokes and puts down into form the request, just for being or calling it into form. So now humans can have all the good intended for them through sacred request, verses through working for money to pay for it.

Humans as the mind of god are the inventers, innovators and artists of Divine Intelligence they are the sacred vessel for Genius and Divine Intelligence. Everything the human needs is intended to be provided for them through the sacred science of manifestation in a magical way an unlimited being with unlimited potential. Omni-awareness is available for all individuals through the sacred heart similar to turning the radio dial to the station one is ready to tune into. As the human becomes conscious of Divine Thought, through the "AHA", they can then bring into form by acknowledgment through the Sacred Mind as Cosmic Sight, and through the Sacred Heart as Divine Understanding.

IGNIGHT YOUR COSMIC SIGHT

Cosmic Re-Cognition, to Re-Ignite Divine Cognition.

Awakened Fohat, Divine Intelligence within and without.

I Claim my Cosmic Sight.

I Claim the Beauty Way, to see beauty and order in everywhere, everyone and everything.

"I see beauty, bountiful, whole, sacred planet earth. Beloved to all cherished and nourished through active expression of this sacred way.

I see my belonging. I see unity,

I envision sacred sanctuary

I am shone divine love, connection, belonging and divine reunion".

COSMIC SIGHT is THE BEAUTY WAY.

Divine Sight, to see the Divinely Intended Beauty, Order and Plan in life through inner and outer-sight.

Out-Picturing. To out-picture is to envision the divinely intended continuously until it is manifested in form.

Pro-Vision is the action of envisioning the completion of a sacred intent as fulfilled and whole. To envision, imagine and see the broken or sick as whole and healed.

The individual creates the experience, manifests into form the experience of "receiving provisions" as they journey through life. Provisions may be staples, supplies, commodities experienced and received in the now, just for being, or in this case for envisioning.

For-Sight & For-See, are to see ahead what may be needed in the now. Forward thinking is thinking ahead. Knowing the answers and solutions needed with ease prior to and in the now.

Pro-Active is taking action to be prepared for the vision as intuitive knowing of possible circumstances.

The individual prepares self for the intuitively known possibility, through the envisioned good.

LIGHT ACTIVATION PLAY-SHEET

DIVINE POWER JUST FOR BEING

It is our inherent power and birth-right to co-create and experience HEAVEN ON EARTH, Just for Being.

 Representing Ray One, a Cosmic Being, the Great Divine Director

Ray I: Divine Will, Illuminated Faith, Power, Protection, Peace, God's First Cause of Perfection.

"We accept our Stewardship as God's & Goddesses Co-Creating the Divine Blueprint of the Highest Intended Good for Mother Earth and all she embodies. Taking back all our Divinely Intended Birthrights and Sacred Power to give birth to new forms freely through the Power of the Spoken Word, Right Action aligned with Divine Will. All Beings are Safe, Protected and Secure through Divine Assurance of Gods Eternal Peace. Establishing Divine Fellowship where each being lifts the other in reverence, esteem, praise, acceptance & inclusion. We Co-Create our Sacred Family, Sacred Community, and Unified Individualized Expression of the ONE."

STANDING IN MY DIVINITY AS MY HIGHER-SELF,

I send my MIGHTY I AM PRESENCE, out ahead of me to remove all obstacles and fulfill each of these Sacred Decrees, Now fulfilling all Divine Intentions both known and unknown prior to me getting there!

Through the POWER OF THE ONE, UNIFIED HEART, the ONE UNIVERSAL TRUTH and the CHRIST IN ME:

I release all soul level contracts and experiences that Power is Force. I release all agreements that I have no choice, but to submit, or be forced to experience the force or will of another.

I place all experiences, and judgments of force as power and of power as abusive or control over another, into the violet flame, to clear the memory, record, cause, core and effect for all incarnations.

I release all soul level contracts, experiences and agreements that I must do something, perform, win, act, control, harden, or play a role to be Safe, Divine, or Worthy. I place all these into the violet flame, to clear the memory, record, cause, core and effect for all incarnations.

I CLAIM FREEDOM AS MY DIVINE BIRTHRIGHT! I take back my Divinely Intended Power to be a Co-Creator Being. I NOW CHOOSE TO CREATE A NEW REALITY.

I NOW Acknowledge SOURCE as Infinite Power within my Sacred Being. Aligned with Divine Will & Might I now Claim and take back ALL the Divinely Intended Powers & Birthrights Spirit intends for me.

I Take back my Divine Power to say NO to all obstacles, blockages, darkness, suffering, hardship, lack, poverty, illness, density or anything, anyone, and any experience that would keep me from my Divinely Intended Good, Birthrights, Fulfillment, Unconditional Love, Unlimited Potential, and Divine Co-Creator Ability to Fulfill the Divine Plan, Blueprint and Joyful Life in Human Form on Mother Earth today and every day!

I Claim my Birthright to remember my Original Souls, Purpose, Origin, Mission, Lessons, vow's and agreements. I remember to remember.

I Declare that my Original Souls, Purpose, Origin, Mission, Lessons, vow's and agreement are now COMPETE, FULFILLED, FINISHED AND DONE! I take back my divine Power to Choose Again, through FREE WILL, JOY and CHOICE.

I Claim FREE WILL and my Birthright to CHOOSE! I Now Choose (24/7) thoughts, behaviors, actions, relationships, locations & experiences that are for my Highest Good and Highest Joy, as is aligned with Divine Will. CHOICE = WILL.

I have the POWER to accept my SACRED DIVINITY and STEWARDSHIP as an UNLIMITED, BEING Co-Creating HEAVEN on EARTH. All Choices I choose are now from my Sacred Heart.

I have the POWER to choose from my SACRED HEART every Divine Intended Experience. Each Choice I choose is immediately co-created into form by the Elemental Kingdom.

I have the POWER to accept the DIVINE PLAN, CREATE the DIVINE PLAN, and FULFILL the DIVINE PLAN through each thought, word and feeling I experience. I NOW CHOOSE thoughts, words, feelings and actions that are DIVINE and for the HIGHEST GOOD.

I open myself to see as God Sees. Thus activating my Divine Understanding of each situation I am involved in. I begin to declare with the Power of the Spoken Word this Divine Awareness by speaking out loud the "Immaculate Concept" of purity and love for and on behalf of family, my friends, Humanity and myself.

I have the POWER to LOVE! I CHOOSE to LOVE.

I have the POWER to FORGIVE. I CHOOSE to FORGIVE.

I have the POWER to be KIND. I CHOOSE to be KIND.

I have the POWER to PRAISE. I CHOOSE to PRAISE.

I have the POWER to experience PEACE. I CHOOSE PEACE.

I have the POWER to experience EASY LIFE. I CHOOSE EASY LIFE.

I have the POWER to experience JOY. I CHOOSE JOY.

I have the POWER to experience BEAUTY. I CHOOSE BEAUTY.

I have the POWER to experience TRUTH. I CHOOSE TRUTH.

I have the POWER to experience ABUNDANCE and INFINITE SUPPLY. I CHOOSE Abundance Consciousness, Infinite Supply and the Divine Demonstration of this Good every day!

I have the POWER to accept that each sacred decree and choice I make can now manifest in form and happen with ease, through physical demonstration and personal experience, JUST FOR BEING.

~ONLY LOVE IS REAL~

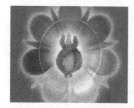

EARTH = HEART.

THE SACRED HEART IS THE ASCENSION CHAMBER AND PORTAL OF ETERNAL BEING.

Through the Sacred Heart, Humans become Cosmic Beings as Solar Sun's in temporary human form. Each being's solar light-body is fully activating shifting consciousness from global to cosmic, universal consciousness in the now.

EMPOWERMENT:

As Empowered Co-Creator Beings, Humans have inherent spiritual birthrights, qualities and virtues. **Inherent** implies our sacred divinity and rights are **Just for Being**, not for doing. Humans are unlimited beings with unlimited potential. Humans as co-creator beings, are intended to fulfill the Divine Plan of Heaven on Earth.

Em-Power-Ment: (three sided triangle)

Em, is to Embody, the reception of divinity and co-creative abilities.	**Power**, is I AM, Being God Goddess in human form.	**Ment**, is Intent, the action of the divinity through conscious choice.

THREE-FOLD FLAME OF SACRED HEART:

LOVE (Pink) Having, Receiving, Left side of heart.	**WISDOM** (Yellow) Here Now, Being, Center of heart.	**POWER** (Blue) Action, Doing, Right side of heart.

HINDU TRINITY: SACRED HEART,

SAT-TAT-AUM: The **BEING.** The **THATNESS.** or **IMMANENCE** and the **WORD** or **HOLY SPIRIT.** Each God has a feminine counterpart or **Shakti,** or **Cosmic Mother**

Brahma, Creator of the Universe, Cosmic Lord Feminine, **Saraswati,** Goddess of Knowledge	**Shiva**, Destroyer of the Universe, Transcendent Godhead, Feminine, **Parvati, (Kali)** Goddess of Power& Transformation.	**Vishnu**, Preserver of the Universe, Cosmic Mind, Feminine, **Lakshimi**, Goddess of Love

SAI BABA: Divinity manifests in the individual as 3 sacred principles. Heart is Ishwara. Mind is Vishnu. Body is Brahma.

1. Principle of ATMA, Absolute Consciousness of Heart or ATMA, gives birth to Mind.
2. Principle of Mind, Cognitive power of mind enables us to cognize inner and outer worlds. **Mind is the fountain head of word and speech.**
3. Principle of Word,

HEART IS THE SEAT OF GOD:	**TWO FORMS OF MEDITATION:**
Word = Brahma, gift of speech.	Joyothi, LIGHT, focus on the flame of a candle, bring into body parts for purification.
Mind = Vishnu embodied as mind.	So-Hum, BREATH, focus attention on breathing: Inhale with" Soooo", Exhale with "Hmmmm".
Heart= Ishwara, (shiva)	

Christ Consciousness is Crystalline Consciousness. The first 3 Rays of Spirit as Crystalline Consciousness:

LOVE & UNDERSTANDING, Ishwara/Shiva & Parvati/Kali: Christ Consciousnessness is developed through the balancing of the threefold flame in the Sacred Heart of Love, Power and Wisdom. Christ or Crystalline consciousness is Being Heart Centered, with an open radiant heart as a fiery vortex of unconditional love, divinely dethatched from personal expectations. The Ruby-Red Ray is the ray of Eternal Transfiguring Love and Christ consciousness. The Divine Life Source is activated and propelled from with-in is an innate urge to become and understand. Ray 2, Anchors in Heart Chakra. Sirius Constellation **ONLY LOVE IS REAL.**

POWER & WILL, Vishnu & Lakshami : Buddha Consciousness is developed through becoming Higher Mind, Divine Intelligence and Understanding as an Eternal Being in temporary human form. It is choosing to live through deliberate conscious intent 24/7 as God Goddess. Understanding that the soul is karmicaly responsible for every thought, feeling and action. It is the Spiritualization of Matter where every molecule or vibration matters. It is choosing, (willing) the divinely intended every moment. Placing the Higher-Self in the decision making or driver's seat. The lower ego mind is the previous self-governing structures that no longer serve the individuals unified good. Ray, 1, Anchors in Crown Chakra. Great Bear Constellation **THE POWER TO CHOOSE LOVE.**

CREATIVE ACTIVE INTELLIGENCE, Brama & Saraswati: Human Form, is the Sacred Temple and vessel of fohat, life force, chi, prana or spirit. The human vessel houses the blueprint and records. It stores the outdated and obsolete, until cleared and upgraded through the aligned union of mind, heart and action. The human being allows for the multidimensional experiences through the causal bodies. The human being is a midwife or transducer, for the activation of mother earth through being a conductor of light or fohat. The co-creator, transcends duality by living with full activation, of unlimited potential, through the three-fold balance of Having, Doing, and Understanding As 13 strands of DNA are fully activated in each actualized individual, the unified ascension of mother earth is fulfilled. Ray, 3, Anchors into the throat chakra. Pleadies Constellation . **CO-CREATING WITH SACRED INTENT, ACTION AND REVERENCE FOR ALL LIFE AS ONE UNIFIED HEART.**

Our **SACRED DIVINITY** is our **INHERIENT BIRTH RIGHT** and is the **Divinely Intended Plan.** Each Human is a Sacred Worthy Being who has *never done anything wrong and never will!* We are inherently SACRED, worthy and *imperfectly perfect,* **JUST FOR BEING!** We are intended to **LIVE WITH EASE**. Humans are intended to live Fully, with Passion, Peace, Joy, Bliss, Purpose and Zeal. **Our SACRED PURPOSE** is to **CO-CREATE HEAVEN ON EARTH** in accompaniment with God's Divine Spiritual Hierarchy. **God's Fiat: is that Man shall have the Gift of Freewill**. As Co-Creator with God, Humans have the authority to invoke the presence and service of the Angelic Hosts thereby liberating all elementals in the co-creation of Heaven on Earth.

It is through the Power of the Spoken Word that Mankind is a Co-Creator Being creating Heaven on Earth. It is through the Activation of Fohat, the Divine Life Source, and the Sacred White Fire of Purity at the center of every atom that Human Masters are able to restore and co-create the Divine Plan. (When Spirit = Electric Fire) merge with (Living Matter = Fire by Friction) it creates Solar Fire or the Activation of the Solar Light Body! Through this Christ Consciousness Soul and Spirit are unified in the Sacred Heart, restoring divine awareness of being Eternal Beings in temporary form. This is the SPIRITUALIZATION OF MATTER.

AFFIRMATIONS: An affirmation is a statement of fact or assertion, usually stated from a place of belief or acceptance. **Firm is from the Latin word to make "firm" or into form.** An affirmation is a way of cognizing the outcome we choose to create or experience. **PLACE HAND ON SACRED HEART WHEN SPEAKING, OR ASKING FOR GUIDANCE.**

Transcending Duality through hand held on sacred heart. Earth=Heart.

1. Placing a Hand on the Heart automatically connects the positive and negative polarities of the mind and heart, much like a copper wire connecting the two sides of a battery. First Ray anchors in Crown Chakra. Second Ray anchors in Heart Chakra
2. Then Speak OUTLOUD. We create through the power of the spoken word. Third Ray anchors in Throat Chakra.
3. Imagine a Golden Orb of Light from your God Self or the God Head, descending into and residing continuously the Sacred Heart.

PLACE HAND ON SACRED HEART AND SPEAK OUT LOUD, THROUGH THE POWER OF THE SPOKEN WORD.

ACTIVATE DIVINE UNDERSTANDING IN SACRED HEART: *"My Higher-Self now resides in me". " Divine Understanding is now activated in me. I Claim my birthright to KNOW, HEAR, and SEE as God Goddess, as Spirit does. I take back my power to Know, See and Hear as God & Goddess does, through my own Sacred Heart, my own Knowing and my own Understanding. I ask my Soul and Higher-Self to be with me today and always. I thank my Soul and Higher-Self for answering all my questions and for showing me my Divine Pathway. I ask this knowledge and guidance to be PHYSICALLY DEMONSTRATED, CLEARLY REVEALED, PLACED IN FROM OF ME, "I ASK GOD FOR THE BURNING BUSH".*

OPEN HEARTED: *"I AM ready to live Open Heartedly. I ask my Higher Self, to remove all heart armor from my Sacred Heart in an easy comfortable way. I Claim my Birthright to live Open Heartedly, My Sacred Heart is a Fiery Vortex of Light. The Sacred Fire is restored in my Sacred Heart and lit at the center of every atom of my Being."*

LIBERATION IN LIGHT: *"I Stand in my Light, Follow Truth from my Heart and Hold up my Torch. My Torch Burns through all Obstacles and Lights my Divinely Intended Pathway! ALL IS REVEALED IN THE LIGHT TODAY! ALL IS LIBERATED IN LIGHT TODAY!"*

FREE WILL, CONSCIOUS CHOICE, FREEDOM. To choose is to will: *"I Claim Free Will as my Divine Birthright! I Claim my Highest Divinely Intended PURIFIED, FREE, SORVIERGN, UNLIMITED,, ETERNAL, MAGICAL BEING in physical and energetic form, In the Now with ease, Inherently just for being!"*

I Claim Choice and take Back my Divine Unlimited Power to Choose Again. I Ask the Angels and Elemental Beings to do this for me." "I take back my Divine Power to Stand! I Stand in my Light. I Stand in Divine Truth. I Stand for Love. I Stand for Truth. I Stand for God. It is safe to Stand in my light, and truth."

CLAIM AND ACTIVATE DIVINE LOVE: *"Divine Love is now activated in me. Divine Love is activated in everyone, everywhere and everything. Divine Love now does its perfect work in me, everyone and everything. I claim my divine birthright to experience infinite abundance".*

"The empowered nourishing mother in her highest divinely intended form, is now activated in the sacred heart of me, everyone and everything."

"I Claim the Highest, Divinely Intended, Eternal, Unconditional Love as my Divine Birthright. I Claim my Being is Inherently Loved, and Worthy just for Being. I open myself to experience an Infinite Supply of Love, Acceptance, Nourishment, Finances, Provisions, and everything that God intends to support my Highest Good. There is Enough! It is Safe to say yes to me and to what is in my sacred heart. I open myself to experience even greater levels of self-love every day. It is safe to feel good. Love is Safe. I AM now Divinely Nourished by everywhere, everyone, and everything. Only Unconditional Love resides in my life today and every day. I Love all people and all people love me, without attachment. Unconditional Love is the only reality I choose to attract in my life. I am now loved by everyone, with ease, just for being. I now experience Unconditional Divine Love in everyone, everywhere and everything. ONLY LOVE IS REAL!"

CLAIM AND ACTIVATE DIVINE WISDOM AND UNDERSTANDING: *"I activate divine wisdom within me. Divine understanding is activated in the sacred heart of me, everyone and everything! I claim my divine birthright to know as God knows. "*

"I now bring into my conscious awareness any energetic (conscious, or unconscious) that is no longer for my highest good. These are now CLEARLY being revealed to me through DIVINE UNDERSTANDING. This process happens with ease, and in a divinely ordered way."

"Divine Understanding is now activated in me and my life. I take back my birthright to know as God, Goddess and Spirit Knows, through my own heart, my own knowing and personal understanding. I Claim Joyful Life as my Divine Birthright. I Claim Easy as my Birthright. I only draw to me life and relationships that are easy and joyful. I take back my power and Birthright to Embrace the Fullness of Life. I AM fully embraced by Life. I AM fully embraced by God. I AM fully embraced by Love. I Claim Safe Sacred Touch as my Birthright. I AM touched by Love. I AM touched by God. I AM touched by everything good. I AM fulfilled by Love. I have the Power to Love. I have the Power to Forgive. I have the power to Choose Again. Only Divine Order now resides in my mind, in my body and in my life. Only Divine Order now resides in all timing. I walk in perfect timing with the Universe."

CLAIM AND ACTIVATE DIVINE POWER: *"Divine Power is activated in me. I take back my divine birthright and power to be free, and to create new realities. I claim my divine birthright to experience eternal peace."*

"I now align myself with the Higher Will of God. Gods will not my own works in and through me, everyone, and everything. Aligning ones will with the higher will of Spirit is the most important thing you can do to become ones highest self on earth!"

"The forgiving father is made alive in me, everyone and everything. The allowing and accepting father is now made alive in me, everyone and everything. The Sacred masculine is now activated resides in the sacred heart of me, everyone, and in everything."

"I Claim my Divine Birthright and open myself to experience all the Divine Power of God Source in my Sacred Heart intended for me. I Claim Free-Will as my Birthright. I Claim my Birthright to Choose. I Choose for my Divine Good. I Claim Freedom as my Divine Birthright. I Claim my Divine Unlimited Potential to give birth to new form freely, and easily. I Claim my Birthright to say NO, I Say no to all

obstacles, blockages, density or anything that would keep me from my Divinely Intended Good. I Claim my Birthright to be Inherently Safe and Protected, just for being. I Claim Eternal Peace as my Divine Birthright. Peace with my past, present and future. I AM at the Center of Eternal Peace."

CLAIM AND ACTIVATE LIGHT: *Light, Light, Light, I AM Light. I Radiate Light, I Amplify Light. I Magnify Light, I Shine Forth my Light. Light is now Produced at the center of my bones and every atom of my being. Light Bursts forth from the center of every cell of my Being. Light, Light, Light, I AM Light.*

ONLY LOVE IS REAL...

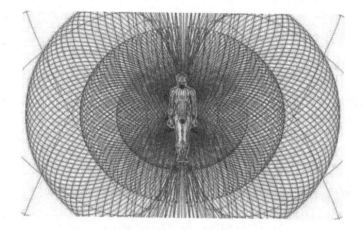

CHAPTER 5

Mastery of the Rays. Co-Creating Gaia's Rainbow Bridge.

RAINBOW CHILD: "As a child I was mesmerized by the rainbow and taught early that each color of the rainbow had an angel and lessen for the process of becoming light, or enlightened. This awareness quickly opened a receptive channel within me to see color and light both when I closed my eyes and with my eyes open around the field of people, plants and animals. I was taught to imagine color or light around others when I experienced discomfort. Mostly I was encouraged to visualize pink or white light around people who were sad, hurt, or angry. Now I realize these simple instructions provided me with a foundation allowing for a healthy intuitive and empathic development that integrated the non-physical spiritual and physical experiences of being an aware and empathic child." Camille Moritz.

BUILDING THE RAINBOW BRIDGE

The Star-Merkaba is our Solar Light Body. Mer = light, Ka = spirit and Ba = body

Ascension is really a descension process. It is the anchoring of the solar light body, or Source Energy from the God-head. Sometimes this is seen in the mind's eye as a Peace Dove entering into the crown.

The **downward flow of light from our Atman,** or God self is a descending spiral of light.

- Imagine and allow a continuous flow of energy/light from the Center of the Sun (central-sun), down through the top of your head, crown chakra, along your spine through the root chakra, down your legs, through the souls of the feet, into the Earth until the diamond core center is filled with energy/light.
- Imagine pyramid of light with the point a foot below the feet and the base above your heart chakra.

The **upward flow of light from the diamond center of earth** is the ascending spiral of light.

- Imagine a continuous flow of energy/light from the Diamond Core Center of Earth up through the souls of the feet, through the root chakra up the spine through the crown chakra and up to the center of the central sun. There is an infinite source of flow available to each of us from these sacred centers.
- Imagine being in a pyramid of light with the point a foot above the head and the base below the solar plexus chakra.

Each pyramid is spinning, one clockwise and the other counter-clockwise. These form a Diamond Light Vortex at the center of the Sacred Heart. At the Center of Peace.

A Star is Born: Light is produced at the center of each atom, electron, & proton, of our Being. Light is produced at the center of the bones, creating the alchemical process of becoming our illuminated radiant golden light being. LIGHT, LIGHT, LIGHT, I AM LIGHT! Merkabah

The Torus, Shri Yantra, Merkaba and Aura are all the same thing!

RAINBOW BRIDGE

Rainbow Bridge, or building the Antakarana, refers to building a strong column of light to the God Head, Source Energy or Atma. This is done through invocation, meditation and mastery of the 7 ray qualities. Keep a constant 24/7 steady spiraling flow both up and down the column of light. This process builds the Antakarana, Rainbow Bridge, sometimes called the Tube of Light. The human is the bridge unifying spirit and matter as the Rainbow.

Once the Soul Invocation has been decreed, God Head or Source Energy will obey thought and move within the physical, emotional, mental bodies and the Aura, this is called evocation. The aura will expand, and radiate luminous colored light.

Invocation: To Invoke is to Decree through the Power of the Spoken Word. It is through the Power of the Spoken Word that Mankind is a Co-Creator Being. The Being Invokes, Source Energy, responds by Evocation. This is a Pouring down of Source Energy into the causal bodies, anchoring the solar light body and building the Rainbow Bridge.

Each time the Soul Invocation is sounded the lines of light projected to the soul and the three aspects of the spiritual triad add strands of light to the creative thread and steadily advances the building of the ANTAHKARANA.

Traditional Theosophical Rainbow Bridge Decree.

RAINBOW BRIDGE INVOKATION:

I AM the SOUL, I AM LIGHT DIVINE, I AM LOVE, I AM WILL, I AM FIXED DESIGN.

INVOKE: I AM THE SOUL

IMAGINE: a line of golden light being projected from the center of you head/ pineal gland straight up through the crown to the soul Star.

EVOKES: Soul Star increases in size, brilliance and radiation and the central channel becomes filled with rainbow fire.

INVOKE: I AM LIGHT DIVINE

IMAGINE: Imagine a line of light bridging to the MENTAL PERMANENT ATOM bridging the concrete and higher abstract mind in the spiritual triad. Permanent Atom will respond with a downpour of light.

EVOKES: Soul Star sends forth a stream of rainbow fire into the central channel.

INVOKE: I AM LOVE

IMAGINE: A line of light reaching for the BUDDIC PERMANENT ATOM, which will respond with a downpour of love energy.

EVOKES: From the heart of the Soul Star is sent down a rose pink energy which floods the central channel.

INVOKE: I AM WILL

IMAGINE: A line of light to the ATMIC PERMANENT ATOM, causing a release of spiritual will.

EVOKES: A royal purple, brilliant clear red, white and indigo blue downpour enters and fills the central channel.

INVOKE: I AM FIXED DESIGN

IMAGINE: knowing from within your souls divine plan. Strengthens the link between abstract mind and the personal self focused in the concrete mind. The downpour relates to your Souls Purpose for this incarnation.

EVOKES: The 7 energy centers along the spine intensify, Magnifies & Identifies our individual specific souls purpose.

Each time the Soul Invocation is sounded the lines of light projected to the soul and the three aspects of the spiritual triad add strands of light to the creative thread and steadily advances the building of the ANTAHKARANA.

Once the Soul Invocation has been said the Soul Star will obey thought and move within the physical, emotional, mental bodies and the Aura. It will expand, contract or send out a beam of energy and radiate various colors of light without conscious direction by you.

Light Meditation: With your hand reach above the head into the soul star, pull down your solar light and place into your crown. Reach up again and pull solar light down into your third eye chakra, next your throat chakra. Now the solar plexus, sacral and root chakra. Next pull down solar light into your knees, feet and below your feet into your earth star. Take time with each reach into your soul star and placing light into each chakra or body part. Let your vessel absorb this intended Solar Light. This meditation will increase your column of light. Over time the column of light will encompass the physical body by increasing in up to 3 feet around the individual.

INDWELLING

Affirmations activate and build the Rainbow Bridge through programing the lower causal bodies of sub-conscious awareness. Through the Power of the Spoken Word, When the human Invokes, **Spirit Evokes**. This means that by Placing ones hand on the sacred heart and speaking out loud, the Higher Self will begin to Put Down these frequencies and fulfill each sacred decree declared. This may be referred to the **Indwelling of the Holy Spirit.**

The human body is a multidimensional vessel for Source to fill, utilize, reside within and work through. Cosmic Light is continuously bathing Mother Earth and her inhabitants. All are receptive to Light. Source as Light continuously descends full-filling the Divine Plan. Humans continuously ascend becoming light as the frequencies increase in the cosmos so do they increase in humans and on the planet.

Humans assimilate source energy through cosmic, electromagnetic, sunlight, breath, food and direct knowing. Source is in continuous co-creation with or with-out awareness. The fountainhead as Source continues to evoke, put-down and fill the multidimensional human with source energy.

The downward cosmic and upward electro-magnetic flows are integrated and expanded through conscious awareness as the Logo's a fohatic fountain of source. Through conscious awareness the human chooses to be divinely aligned with source energy. This alignment allows the vessel to assimilate the maximum amount of source energy.

If the human vessel is contaminated through toxic choices, foods, air, thoughts, emotions, traumas, programs or unconscious records, Divine Fulfillment is prevented. These places are 'blown up' as the light frequencies descend and increase, causing physical damage, disease and many outer manifestations of unfulfilling life. Through conscious awareness the human becomes the **Master of Being.** Through mastery, undesired life experiences and mis-qualified creations are let-go, freed and transmuted. Through mastery the Divine Plan is Activated, Restored and Co-Created as Heaven on Earth. The Seven Ray Lessons are the lessons of Self-Mastery.

I Let-Go of all that no longer serves me.

I am my Highest Divinely Intended Free Purified expression of God Goddess in human form.

I assimilate the maximum amount of Source Energy intended for me with ease.

All is purified in my life with east. I am Divinely Fulfilled with ease, just for being.

MASTERY OF HUE-MAN BEING

DIVINE ORDER, DIVINE INTELLIGENCE, DIVINE LOGOS.

Logos in Greek means "Logic" or more literally the "word, statement or argument for reasoning" In other words, Logos is using logic or reasoning to voice, express and convey the Ordered Intelligence of Spirit. In Christianity "Logos" has been referred to as the second in the holy trinity known as Christ. In Sufism, no contact between God and man can be made without the Logos. In computer programing classes "Logos" is a programing language for computers.

"The Being which Naught can be said" is known as the Fountain Head and the Cosmic Logos. Fohat, the electrical life force of Divine Intelligence as Infinite Spirit, is downloaded, activated, assimilated, integrated, understood and expressed through Logos as the reasoning Word and Mind of God Goddess, by human's who are Christ Being's.

> *"I AM THE MIND OF GOD GODDESS", "I AM THE WORD OF GOD GODDESS", "I AM THE WISDOM OF GOD GODDESS", "I KNOW AS GOD KNOWS" I UNDERSTAND THE DIVINELY INTENDED PLAN" "I SPEAK AS GOD SPEAKS" "I SPEAK THE DIVINELY INTENDED PLAN INTO FORM THROUGH THE POWER OF THE SPOKEN WORD AS A CO-CREATOR CHRIST BEING." "I AM THE LOGOS OF GOD GODDESS".*

The Seven Rays of Spirit are a repetitive pattern of logos or divinely ordered intelligence. Source as Divine Intelligence is an Infinite Field of Possibilities that is channeled or known through the spectrums of the electromagnetic fields known as frequencies, rishis, rays, sounds, colors, octaves, light, angels, guides and many other vibrational conduits.

Divinely Ordered Intelligence repeats itself through all dimensions and levels of awareness. The macrocosm is a mirror or reflection of the microcosm. Light refracts infinity yet remains light. The Macrocosm and the Microcosm mirror each other as all are one and Source flows through all.

The Ray Lessons allow the human to conceptualize ideas that transcend the duality of global consciousness into awakened cosmic awareness as ONE Source with individuated expressions. Multi-Dimensional Hue-Mans. The human body is a transducer of Source Intelligence. It is a conduit of the infinite field of Source Intelligence as Light, Energy and Frequency also known as our Unlimited Potential's.

The Ray teachings are a road map of consciousness for the path of ascension. Humans as multi-dimensional beings hold within them an energetic system of causal bodies, meridians, chakras, biological, chemical, cellular, and DNA intelligences. These energetic systems are a reflection of the whole, including cosmic, celestial and multi-universal consciousness. These are energetic channels allowing the Rays of Spirit as Logos to individuate through the Galaxy, Solar Systems, Planet's, Human mind, body and spirit.

This process in humans is a receptive and expanding awareness of consciousness, increasing the Light Quotient and activating the Divine Blueprint of Dormant Potentials, Divine Virtues and Divine Super-Powers held within the biology at the micro level and in the Cosmos at the Macro level. The ray teachings, provide a system of guidance for multidimensional being. The human has the choice to become a conscious director of Divine Intelligence as a Conscious Co-Creator with the Celestial Hosts and Source Energy.

THE SEVEN RAYS OF GOD,

In traditional Theosophical Ray Teachings. Each of the rays has a form of teaching truth to humanity. "The seven rays are the sum total of the Divine Consciousness of the Universal Mind". They are also referred to as the seven universes or star systems who's light, vibrational frequencies or rays influence Mother Earth through cosmic radiation.

They might be thought of as seven intelligent fohatic or electric spirits though whom the Divinely Intended Plan is working out. They embody divine purpose, and express the qualities required for materializing this purpose. The Rays create the forms and are the forms through which the divine idea can be carried forward to completion. The Rays or rishis may be regarded as the brain of the Divine Intelligence or Source Energy.

The rays correspond to the seven causal bodies, seven dimensions, seven chakras, seven colors of the rainbow, seven music notes and to the seven major glands which determine the quality of the physical body. Each Ray has a vibration or frequency through each dimension. They are conscious executers of divine purpose. They are the seven breaths, animating all forms which have been created by them to carry out the Divinely Intended Plan.

Each of the rays have corresponding angels, guides, totems, lessons and frequencies. Learning which guides work with each of the rays will help one to gain guidance for self-mastery and fulfillment of the Divine Plan.

The Seven Stars of the Great Bear are the originating source of the seven rays of the Milky Way Galaxy. Each ray is an individualized aspect or frequency of the "Fountainhead" or Source Energy. The Great Bear is identified in theosophy as the "Planetary Logos, the Great Being or Heavenly Man".

Mother Earth resides with-in the Milky Way Galaxy. Mother Earth as a Live Being receives Cosmic Light from each of these seven stars. Humans as Earth Beings also receive light from these seven stars.

Cosmic Light as the individualized aspects of source, are "inherent potentials". Source is expressed through each solar system, star, planetary body and human chakra system. This is a "Stepping Down" of Source Energy" or Divine Consciousness into denser dimensions as Divine Intelligence. Each person is a part of the Divine Plan for the Universe and the seven ray's link and blend all human and sentient beings to fulfill this Divine Plan.

According to Wikpedia, (in-part) *"The united energies of the three constellations the Great Bear, The Pleiades and Sirus which control and energize our solar system work through the medium of the seven rays and these in turn express themselves through the twelve constellations which form the zodiac wheel. They are then embodied in the seven sacred planets and are represented on earth by the seven Spirits before the Throne of God. (the symbol of synthesis) When these energies reach our planet a combination of three groups of energetic patterns from rays, planets and zodiacal signs is formed. They find their way through the major vortexes, chakras, cities of mother earth and through the human race."*

The first three Rays are called the **Rays of Aspect.** An Aspect is a particular part or feature of something. Meaning the first three rays of God are the primary features of Source known as God Goddess.

The first three rays are receptive to the Divine Plan. Meaning the human is, The Sun or Light of God. A "Solar Sun" Shining bright, revealing the divine plan, knowing the divine plan, materializing the divine plan, and being the divinely intended. The "Hue-Man" is a receptive vessel for inherent qualities, virtues and potentials of Source that actualizes these qualities as the Divine Plan.

THE FIRST THREE RAYS OF ASPECT

Ray One is the Great Bear Ursa Major which is the Planetary Head Center. The Manu. Plane of Divinity. The first ray, Will and Power is the highest plane called Adi, the Logoic Plane of the Solar System. Anchored, Activated, and Known in the Crown Chakra and Pineal Gland. Will dynamically applied, emerges in manifestation of power. Ray one embodies the dynamic idea of God and thus the Most High starts the work of creation.

Ray Two is the Constellation Sirius which is the Planetary Heart Center. The Christ. Plane of Monad. The second Ray, Love and Wisdom is the Monadic Plane. Anchored, Activated, Expressed and Known in the Heart Chakra and Thymus Gland. Love, magnetically functioning, produces wisdom. Ray two is occupied with the first formulations of the plan upon which the form must ve constructed and the idea materialized. The blueprints come into being with their mathematical accuracy, their structural unity and their geometrical perfection. This is the ray of the Master Builder.

Ray Three is the Pleiades which is the Planetary Throat Center. The Maha-Chohan. Plane of Spirit & Atma. The third ray is Creative Active Intelligence, the plane of Spirit or Atma. Anchored, Activated, Expressed and Expressed through the Throat Chakra and Thyroid Gland. Intelligence, potentially found in substance, causes activity. Ray three constitutes the active building forces. The great architect with his builders who organizes the material, starts the work of construction and eventually materializes the idea and purpose of god through god the Sun as hue-man.

The human is receptive to the Divine Plan through the higher causal bodies as being the Love, Power and Wisdom of God Goddess. A process of Creative Active Intelligence, which may be defined as Logos or the consciousness awareness of being God Goddess and co-creating divinely intended order through multidimensional expression of the sacred mind, sacred heart and sacred body as one unified love.

The first three rays, Love Power and Wisdom of Spirit are actualized through the four elemental causal bodies of matter and the human form as inherent virtue's or attributes of sacred being known as the Divine Plan or Heaven on Earth.

Seven Rays expressed and actualized through Senses Human-Being.

Touch, 1st Ray, Regeneration, Destruction. The Hand of God
Intuition, 2nd Ray, Love-Wisdom. The Understanding of God
Sight, 3rd Ray, Vision. The Eye of God
Smell, 4th Ray, Art. The Beauty of Revelation
Intellect, 5th Ray, Mind. The Knowledge of God
Taste, 6th Ray, Idealism. The Desire of Community
Hearing, 7th Ray, Magic. The Word of Power

The Rays of Attribute Actualize the Divine Plan.

Rays four through seven are called the **Rays of Attribute**. An attribute is a quality or feature that is regarded as a character or inherent part of someone or something. Each eternal soul incarnating as a human co-creator has inherent birthrights that are intended just for being.

The human as god goddess expresses, creates, gives life, births life, materializes life, manifests life and actualizes life just for being. Every thought, feeling and action is the fountainhead of source, over spilling with new experience's known as life or form. As all vibration creates form. So every thought, feeling and action is creating what it is. The Rays of Attribute actualize as the divinely intended birthrights, qualities and potentials that are inherent for all who claim them as aligned with the one unified heart.

The conscious human who chooses to be as god. "I am Like God" the first ray. Through the activation of Divine Understanding. 'I am the understanding of god" the second ray. Actively and intelligently choosing Love. "I am the Love of God" the third ray. This human is the progenitor of the divine plan in earthily form.

Rays of Attribute, the Four Minor Rays.

The Rays of Attribute are rays four through seven and correspond to the *four lower causal bodies of matter/humans*. The four rays of attribute find their synthesis through the third ray of aspect. **The rays of attribute express themselves equally on all planes.**

Expression through the KINGDOMS IN NATURE:

Ray IV, Harmony, conflict, 4th Kingdom, Human/ The Balance

Ray V, Concrete Knowledge, 3rd Kingdom, Animal

Ray VI, Devotion, 2nd Kingdom, Vegetable

Ray VII, Ceremonial Ritual, 1st kingdom, Mineral

The Four Rays of Attribute express themselves through man as:

Ray IV, Harmony, Conflict, Physical Body, earth.

Ray V, Concrete Knowledge, Etheric Body, fire.

Ray VI, Devotion, Astral Body, water.

Ray VII, Ceremonial Ritual, Mental Body, air.

The Rays of Attribute

Ray Four, Harmony through Conflict. Activated, Anchored and Actualized in Root Chakra and Adrenal Glands. Plane of Intuition, Buddhic plane. Ray four is the plane of Buddhi or Intuition. It is the midway point where all energies flowing from the higher and lower triads meet.

Finding Light, one now sees light and visions of greater brilliance. This now becomes the object of search. One has mastered the uses of duality and has learned to at-one soul and body into one instrument for spirit.

Ray Five is Concrete Knowledge and Analytical Science. Activated, Anchored and Actualized in Third Eye Chakra and Pituitary Gland. Mental Plane. Ray five is a Mental Plane blending of rays one and three. This is the Plane of the Soul, higher and lower minds.

Triple Aspects of Mind:

1. Abstract of higher mind, the embodiment of a higher triad.

2. The concrete of lower mind, the highest aspect of the lower self.

3. The ego or solar Angel, the purified Light Mind, Who expresses intelligence, both abstractly and concretely and is the point of unification. This ray is a pure channel for divine will. Choice = Will.

Ray Six is the ray of Devotion and Idealism. Activated, Anchored and Actualized in Solar Plexus Chakra and Pancreas. Ray six is the astral or emotional plane and is linked with the center of emotional energy in humans in the Solar Plexus. It is the ray of personal love aspiration desire and religion. Through this ray personal emotions and desires are lifted into purified emotions and aspirations.

Ray Seven is the ray of Ceremonial Order, Ritual and Magic. Activated, Anchored and Actualized in Sacral Chakra and Gonads or Ovaries. Ray seven is the seventh plane called the physio-etheric plane or the plane of ordered service and ceremonial activity. Ray of purification and transmutation clearing the records of the soul for new life.

RAY LESSONS FOR BECOMING AN ANGELIC HUE-MAN.

Ray 1, Will & Power. Anchors into the Crown. Pineal Gland.

It is Gods will that Humans are co-creators of the Divine Plan. Humans are inherently empowered to fulfill this Divine Purpose. Humans have the Power to Choose. Humans are intended to have Free Will and Free Choice. Humans are intended to be safe and fully protected in the purpose of co-creating the divine plan. Humans are intended to experience eternal peace as the Peace of God. Being at the Center of Peace.

The Divine Plan is illuminated, known and revealed with-in the sacred-heart. At the Center of Peace. Illuminated Faith is experienced when human thoughts and feelings are aligned. In Faith ("by feeling as if") miracles happen easily and just for being. Belief is a Super-Power. Through belief, Spontaneous Healing and Manifesting happens in the Now. The Will, Power, Purpose and Protection of God is the intended Power of Humans.

Humans have the right to "Say No", to any obstacle or impediment to fulfilling the Divine Plan. The Power to Undo, Let-Go, Release, Revoke and Rescind is an inherent right for humans through the power to choose.

That which the Human Chooses is also willed into form through Inherent Gods Power. Humans are responsible for all choices. The Human has the power to choose that which is aligned with Divine Will and the power to ask the Divine Plan to be revealed, made known and understood within the sacred heart and sacred mind.

Ray 2, Love & Wisdom. Anchors into the Heart. Thymus Gland.

The Heart Chakra is our Divine Center. An Open Radiant Heart is a Crystalline Heart. It allows us to access all unconscious, past, future, and current wisdom we would like to know. This wisdom is revealed to our inner knowing by asking with intent. The Heart is where the multidimensional being unifies into the one unified truth. A simple way to be heart centered is to place your hand on your heart, while requesting information, setting intention or sending healing.

One must balance the three-fold flame of Love Power and Wisdom in the Sacred Heart. The Sacred Heart Understanding is activated and made known through the Power of the One Unified Heart. Known also as The Law of One. The Higher-Self becomes the Divine Director of the human being.

Through the merging of the upper and lower triads. The lessons of duality are transcended by healing the wounds of betrayal. Separation from God Gender inequality, miss-use of power lack of understanding or wisdom. Inner species conflicts from various human and non- human lifetimes.

Through empowered understanding as an eternal soul, god goddess in temporary human form, the human frees all karmic history, builds the antakarana, activate the solar-light body and becomes the Solar-Christ co-creating the Divine Plan as Heaven on Earth.

Ray 3, Creative Active Intelligence. Anchors in the throat. Thyroid Gland.

Humans have the Power to Co-Create through the Power of the Spoken Word. All sound vibrates, creating form. Every word a human thinks or speaks is actively being created through the elemental order of the universe. Humans are responsible for every thought, word, feeling and action they experience. Humans have the Power to Free, Release and Un-do, or Destroy any experienced identified as not serving the Law of One.

The human is the creative active expression of source through Divine Knowing, Divine Understanding and Divine Action. The throat chakra will store self-limitations and judgments against the self. The throat chakra also stores energetics of being over-powered and controlled by others. The throat is the Mouth of God. Humans are the Word of God. Humans are gods genius, inventors as the action, intelligence, and voice of creator. The Zeal of God is activated in the throat chakra.

Ray 4, Harmony through Conflict. Anchors in Root. Adrenal Glands.

After the human has aligned the three-fold flame in the sacred heart, of Love, Power and Wisdom, the human is propelled into the Fourth Ray Lesson of learning how to create harmony in all places of conflict and discord. This process activates the Kundalini known as the Goddess Shakti, in the Root Chakra. Divine Life Source is released and raised up the spine to clear the remaining akashic records, misaims and distortions not of the Divinely Intended Plan.

The Conscious human begins to become the vessel of transmutation by **lifting** to God Source all concerns, worries and less than intended experiences. Raising up, bringing into the light and revealing all disharmonious experiences through self-love, self-acceptance and self-empowerment.

The fourth Ray is considered the Ascension Ray or Mother Flame. The Sacred White Fire is lit at the center of the bones and every atom to burn through and purge the body/matter of the records/programs of limitation. The fire is ignited with-in 'fire letters'. The human's purpose is in part to create harmony everywhere one has or is experiencing strife, struggle. ONLY LOVE IS REAL, all conflict is an illusion, or repetitive program of limitation, bondage and hellish life.

Ray 5, Concrete Knowledge & Science. Anchors in Third Eye. Pituitary Body.

The Fifth Ray of Spirit is the ray of concrete and abstract knowledge. There is no separation between science and religion or philosophy as each is a method of understanding the "Divinely Ordered Intelligent Universe. The fifth ray holds the Divine Blueprint. Divine Healing and Restoration of the Divine Plan happens through the third eye as the human begins to see, visualize, imagine, envision, out-picture and affirm the Beauty and Order of Source Intelligence.

In the veils of illusion, the individual may experience having no choice or being controlled by an external force. The human mind may be filled with the thought forms and programs of other people's cognitions, beliefs or of false inorganic programs implanted or overlaid on the individual from imposter spirits and archonic entities.

In Illumination the individual understands the divinely ordered science of co-creating an alternative solution as an unlimited being of source energy, through free-will, thought, choice, feeling, vibration and activation. One healing method is to Beam a green ray of light out ones third eye continuously, this lifts the physical world into order and beauty.

Ray 6, Devotion & Idealism. Anchors in Solar Plexus. Pancreas.

Ray six is the astral or emotional plane and is linked with the center of emotional energy in humans in the Solar Plexus. It is the ray of personal love aspiration desire and devotion. Through this ray personal emotions and desires are lifted into purified emotions and aspirations. The solar plexus is the center of peace when the human has faith in their power and purpose to fulfill the Sacred Plan.

Ray six is the spiritual lesson of always choosing the highest intended choice in each moment for the higher-self unified with ONE-HEART. Choosing the path of devotion to becoming like god as god. Choosing to love the humans self as divine in every experience moment and circumstance. Devoting oneself in body mind and spirit to the highest idea, blueprint or possibility. Choosing peace at the center of peace as the light and glory of God Goddess. Transmuting dense experiences by raising them to spirit through love and light.

Ray 7, Ceremonial Order, Ritual & Magic. Anchors in Sacral. Gonads.

The Seventh Ray is the ray of mastery, transmutation, ceremony, magic and ritual. It is through "Continuous Daily Self-Care Routines" that the individual gains self-mastery. A practice of constant daily routines or rituals build a strong energetic foundation for anchoring of the Solar Light Body. Continual personal rituals of devotion, self-mastery and transmutation are birthed into form through the individual's power to un-manifest, or delete the outdated forms and birth the new transmuted forms, in freedom, choice and pleasure.

Each ray has the sacred white fire or seed of purity within and holds a Spiritual Lesson and Guidance for co-creating the Divine Plan. These seeds are inherent spiritual qualities and virtues held within the unlimited potentials of every human who chooses to align with source energy. The seventh ray magically brings purifies through the fire of transmutation freeing the soul from illusion, strife, obstacles and any impediment from Self-Mastery and Freedom as a Magical Being.

The 8ᵗʰ Ray transcends the third dimension and may be referred to as the Sacred White Fire or Platinum Ray of Quickening.

In this quickening process of awakening one begins to become conscious of a multi-dimensional awareness that extends beyond what one has been instructed as a third dimensional world of linear time and space. All the human senses become heightened through this natural increase in frequency. In this increased awareness the individual may begin to "see into alternative dimensions or parallel realities". Some begin to see the aura, color around people, plants and animals. Some have dreams of apocalyptic times or of giving birth to a golden child. Many individuals my leave a long time relationship or pick up and move to a new location. Many begin to see through the lies and distortions of the "old control system" a parasitic control system that has been referred to as the fear matrix, illuminati, cabal, dark forces, the devil, reptilian agenda, 1%, and other terms.

Eventually awareness of personal empowerment increases allowing one to transcend the lower vibrational matrix of fear based consciousness. In fear based consciousness the individual makes life choices based on avoiding fearful possibilities. The new matrix of Unlimited Potential, is a paradigm shift, that allows the individual to become a conscious co-creator in a life where Everything in the Universe is Conspiring to Support, Uplift, Energize, Vitalize and Provide for the Beings Inherent rights according to the Divinely Intended Plan of the fifth dimensional life matrix. It is through the Fiat of God, that each human is intended to have free will and be an Unlimited Crystalline Christ co-creating the Divine Plan through human form on Earth.

LIGHT ACTIVATION PLAY-SHEET

KARMIC BOARD OF RECORD KEEPERS

A group of eight ascended masters and cosmic beings
who dispense justice to this system of worlds, adjudicating
karma, mercy and judgment on behalf of every soul.

Place Hand on Sacred Heart and Speak out Loud:

 Representing Ray 1, A Cosmic Being, The Great Divine Director

Ray 1: Divine Will, Illuminated Faith, Power, Protection, God's First Cause of Perfection.

We accept our Stewardship as God's & Goddesses Co-Creating the Divine Blueprint of the Highest Intended Good for Mother Earth and all she embodies. Taking back all our Divinely intended Birthrights and Sacred Power to give birth to new forms freely through the Power of the Spoken Word, Right Action aligned with Divine Will. All Beings are Safe, Protected and Secure through Divine Assurance of Gods Eternal Peace. Establishing Divine Fellowship where each being lifts the other in reverence, esteem, praise, acceptance & inclusion. We Co-Create our Sacred Family, Sacred Community, and Unified Individualized Expression of the ONE.

The Divine Life Force is now Activated in me, everywhere, everyone and everything, to bring forth all that inspires, motivates, energizes, or serves the Highest Good. I take back my power to live and die freely through joy, choice and dignity!

Representing Ray 2, Ascended Lady Master, The Goddess of Liberty

Ray 2: Enlightenment, Wisdom, Illumination, Understanding, Perception and Constancy

Divine Understanding is now Activated in the Hearts and Minds of all Beings.

I Choose to Stand in my Light, Follow Truth from my Sacred Heart, Hold up my Torch. This Torch burns through all obstacles and lights my Divinely Intended Pathway!

My Higher Self now resides in me & my Heart, Divine Understanding is Activated in me. I take back my power of Divine Revelation, to Know & See as God Goddess knows and sees, through my own heart, understanding, and knowing.

Each time I ask from my Sacred Heart, a Divine Answer is Always revealed through Physical Demonstration, through my own knowing and understanding.

I call forth ALL to be clearly revealed and understood in the light of Diamond Consciousness, All secrets, betrayal, injustice, corruption, misinformation , hidden agendas, manipulation or anything that is not aligned with Gods Divinely Intended Good is now clearly revealed, and brought forth into the light, through Divine Justice, Freedom and Liberation!

I Claim my Infinite, Eternal, Cosmic Being! I Claim Immortality as my Birthright! I Claim my Royal Heritage as God Goddess in Human Form.

Representing Ray 3, Ascended Master Lady Nada

Ray 3: Transfiguring Divine Love, Adoration, Reverence for All Life and Tolerance.

"Behold my Beloveds; I come to you this day in the Spirit of Divine Love. The transformation is upon you, and it is time for the awakening of consciousness to the knowledge of the one truth. 'ALL IS ONE, ONE IS ALL.'"

All is made Whole, Each Being's original purpose, mission or soul's contracts are now fulfilled and complete. It is time to Choose again through the Sacred Heart of Infinite Joy and Bliss.

I open myself to receive all the infinite supply and good fortune intended for me. I am now Divinely Nourished by everywhere, everyone, and everything.

I open myself to experience the completion and fulfillment of my Highest Good.

Divine Transfiguring Love is now activated in me, in everyone, everywhere and everything. I love all people and all people love me without attachment…

Divine Reverence & Tolerance is now activated I the Hearts and Minds of all Beings to bring forth Divine Love, Acceptance and Unity.

I now recognize and utilize all Mother Earth's resources through Divine Reverence, Gratitude and Harmony. This Reverence is now activated in all Beings through the Unified One.

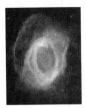

Representing Ray 4, The Elohim Cyclopea

Ray 4: The Ascension Flame, the Immaculate Concept, Purity, Restoration, and Resurrection.

I Claim my Highest Divinely Intended Purified, Restored and Resurrected, Fifth Dimensional Vibrational Form in the Now!

Standing in my Divinity, as my Higher-Self, I now choose to hold thoughts of purity and love for and on behalf of family, my friends, mankind and myself. I choose to practice the act of the "IMMACULATE CONCEPT". In this process whenever I experience fear or undesirable qualities in a friend, family or situation, I recognize this situation and hold beside it, pure thoughts of what I would like to experience, or what God sees as the divinely intended idea, blueprint, or possibility. To do this I open myself to see as God Sees. Thus activating my Divine Understanding of each situation I am involved in. I begin to declare with the Power of the Spoken Word this Divine Awareness by speaking out loud the "Immaculate Concept" for each situation.

The Sacred White Fire is lit and activated in me, my life, and everything in my world to burn through all that no longer serves.

Representing Ray 5, The Goddess of Truth, Pallas Athena

Illuminated Truth, Healing, Consecration, Concentration, and Inner Vision

I Claim Divine Truth as my birthright. I open myself to know Divine Truth, Have Divine Truth and Reveal Divine truth through my Sacred Heart. I always choose for my Highest Good from my Sacred Heart.

I Claim Diamond Consciousness as my birthright. I AM the Mind of God.

I see each and every person, situation and event as God See's it or intends it to be. I see wholeness, beauty and divine order in everyone, everywhere and everything.

Only Divine Order now resides in me and my life. I walk in Perfect Timing with the Universe; I am always in the right place at the right time.

Representing Ray 6, The Goddess of Justice and Opportunities, Ascended Lady Master Portia

Ray 6: Divine Grace, Healing, Devotional Worship, and Peace.

I Claim Eternal Peace as my Birthright. I Am at Peace with my past, present and future. I AM at the Center of Peace. Eternal Peace is now activated in the Hearts and Minds of All Beings to bring forth Harmony, Balance and Joy.

God's Divine Justice is now activated in and resides through all government's, organizational systems, educational systems, corporations, technology, military, and all governing systems to bring forth Eternal Peace, Divine Order, Divine Equality, and the Highest Good of the One Unified Heart!

DIVINE REFORM AND FREEDOM FOR ALL BEINGS!

 **Representing Ray 7, The Goddess of Mercy, Kuan Yin**

Ray: 7 Freedom, Liberty, Justice, Victory, Mercy, Compassion, Forgiveness, and Transmutation.

I Claim Divine Forgiveness as my Birthright, I now allow myself to be forgiven for all lifetimes human and non-human. I am open to forgiving all unforgivable acts of everyone everywhere.

I Claim Freedom today and Every day. I Claim my Good today and every day! I Claim Success today and every day and I Claim Victory in all of these!

Divine Freedom is now activated in the Hearts and Minds of all Beings.

I call forth Lady Quan Yin asking Spirit to lift all pain, suffering, hardship, burden, obligation, anger, regret, embarrassments, shame or any other heavy experience to now be lifted through the Grace and Forgiveness of God, allowing balance, harmony, peace and wholeness to be fully restored to my Being.

I open myself to have Divine Compassion, Forgiveness, and Tolerance for all Beings.

All is now transmuted in the Violet Flame! I AM a Being of Violet Fire; I AM the Purity Spirit Desires! I AM the Violet Flame in me Burning out of Purity!

Representing Ray 8, Vajrakilya, Spokesman of the five Dyani Buddha's

Clarity, Divine Perception, and Discernment.

I Claim Divine Clarity, Perception and Discernment as my Birthright; I open myself to know as God Goddess Knows.

I place all experiences or ignorance, anger, hatred, pride, misery, desire, lust, jealousy, and fear into the violet flame to clear the memory, record, cause, core, and effect for all time.

I Claim Divine Enlightenment, affirming, Light, Light, I AM Light! Light is produced at the center of my bones and bursts forth from the center of every molecule, proton and electron of my multi-dimensional Being.

I Claim my Golden Heritage, Golden Consciousness and Golden Birthrights.

Christ Consciousness is Crystalline Consciousness.

Mother Earth as Living Planet of One now ascends in frequency to become a Crystalline 12th dimensional planet of Crystalline Christ Consciousness. The 12 Cosmic Rays are not linear, they are exponential. The 12 Cosmic Rays are inherent potentials or virtues held within the fire center, known as the fire letters, of every atom and the DNA and RNA of multi-dimensional being.

The 7 rays provide guidelines for third dimensional linear time teaching humans the lessons of living as One Human Race through the One Unified Global Heart.

The 12 Cosmic Rays of the Solar Hierarchy, provide guidelines for higher dimensional awareness and activation of the Divine Plan.

Through the Cosmic Consciousness of a unified Universal Brotherhood and Sisterhood. Eternal Beings incarnating in and out of form for the experience of individuation as Free Sovereign Beings. Consciously choosing and joining intent freely to co-create the Highest Idea in Form. Heaven on Earth aligned with the One Divine Mind and Heart of Love.

12 Solar Aspects of Deity

Theosophical teachings refer to the Twelve Hierarchies of the sun, each having 144 thousand cosmic beings in service and each of the cosmic beings has 144 thousand angels at their command.

The 12 Hierarchies are represented at the Court of the Sacred Fire on Sirius by the four and twenty elders, twelve sets of twin-flames. These 12 are depicted on a clock or circle. The same as the 12 astrological signs or a horoscope.

Traditional theosophical mystery schools assign corresponding ascended masters, elohim and angels for each clock line as follows.

12, Capricorn,	The Great Divine Director And The Seven Archangels.
1, Aquarius	Saint Germain And The Angelic Hosts Of Light
2, Pisces,	Jesus And The Great Hosts Of Ascended Masters
3, Aries,	Helios And The Great Central Sun Magnet
4, Taurus,	God Obedience And The Seven Might Elohim
5, Gemini,	El Morya And The Legions Of Mercury
6, Cancer	Serepis Bey And The Great Seraphim And Cherubims
7, Leo,	Goddess Of Liberty And The Lords Of Karma
8, Virgo,	Lord Lanto And The Lords Of Wisdom
9, Libra,	Might Victory And The Lords Of Individuality
10, Scorpio,	Cyclopea And The Lords Of Form
11, Sagittarius,	Lord Matreya And The Lords Of Mind

The Cosmic Clock identifies the Divine Virtue of each of the Solar Hierarchies, the astrological correspondance and the aligned chakra of the body temple. These are the virtues of crystalline consciousness. Providing a map for mastery. Divine alignment, unifying the sacred heart and sacred mind with Source. Mastering each of the 12 divine virtues completes the experience of duality. I call this stepping of the wheel of Karma. It activates 12 or more strands of DNA and transcends the soul into the experience or Magical Being through the power of the 13. Where heavenly life is easily manifested just for being.

> "The twelve hierarchies of the sun are cosmic beings of light, also known as the Twelve Solar Hierarchies. They focus certain aspects of God's consciousness through the constellations. Although these beings are known by the names of the zodiac, the groups of stars in these configurations are not the Hierarchy. They simply use these and other stars to release their energy. Your causal body has focal points for the release of this energy and how you use it can make a big difference in your life. There are twelve lines on the zodiac. Each line symbolizes a God-quality as well as the tests that must be overcome. On each line of the clock is an ascended master who lowers into manifestation one of the twelve qualities of the solar hierarchy. The spiritual path is the path of self-transformation and personal growth. It involves inner

healing and rites of passage. The ascended masters are our teachers
who give us our initiations and exams. Karma is a Sanskrit word
meaning, "act," "action," "word," or "deed." The sages of old have long
taught about the precision of karma. They say all life is energy. Daily
we are deciding how to use it. We either put a positive or a negative
spin on it by our by our thoughts, words and deeds. Karma is the
universal law of cause and effect. It states that all energy we send forth
will eventually return to us. The science of the Cosmic Clock is based
on the law of cycles and can be used to chart the cycles of karma. We
begin at the twelve o'clock line under the hierarchy of Capricorn and
continue in a clockwise direction. In divine astrology all things begin
in Capricorn." yourcosmicclock.com

On a clock Face place each listed.

12:00	Crown. Capricorn. Power of God
1:00	Seat of the Soul. Aquarius. Love of God
2:00	Solar-Plexus. Pisces. Mastery of God
3:00	Heart. Aries, Control of God
4:00	Third Eye, Taurus. Obedience of God
5:00	Throat, Gemini, Wisdom of God
6:00	Base of Spine. Cancer. Harmony of God
7:00	Seat of the Soul. Leo. Gratitude of God
8:00	Solar Plexus. Virgo. Justice of God
9:00	Heart. Libra. Reality of God
10:00	Third-Eye. Scorpio. Vision of God.
11:00	Throat. Sagitaurius. Victory of God.

Meditative Exercise. An individual who has their astrological natal chart, can place the chart over the Solar Hierarchy graph and learn how this hierarchy is influencing ones soul process in this incarnation. Place hand on the sacred heart and ask members of the Solar hierarchy to come forward thorough one's own inner knowing with messages and guidance for fulfilling ones Soul Purpose. Remember messages are revealed through the language of the soul in symbolism, metaphor, synchronicity, and coincidence. Also through the extrasensory perceptions in returning wisdom to self through external bodies of wisdom already studied and integrated within.

Keepers of the Flame, Activator's of the Purified Upgraded Divine Plan in the Now.

Anchoring the Light Body is a natural process of increased frequency. Ascension is a Descension process of systematically anchoring the Light Body through Increasing the Quotient of Light held within the Center of every Atom. This process also builds the Antakarana, Rainbow Bridge or Column of Light to Source Energy. Activating the Solar Light Body and propelling the soul into Crystalline (Christ-like) Being or Cosmic Consciousness.

Each one of the 12 dimensions can be thought of as a spectrum of solar hierarchy, archetypes, inherent virtues, or seed potentials held with-in the 12 strands of DNA. These inherent virtues repeat themselves through each frequency, ray and through the threefold nature of being.

Christ Conscious is obtaining mastery within the fullness of 12 dimensions of consciousness and unifying through the ONE Global Heart. Earth is intended to be a 12 D planet. The shift from 12 to 13 strand DNA activation is a transcendence that may be experienced as a Paradigm Shift. Instant manifestation as miracles are activated in the 13 dimensions of Magical Being.

The 12 aspects of Solar Deity are the inherent and intended virtues and qualities that all humans are intended to have, be and experience through the Divine Plan. Each is an aspect of purity held at the center of each molecule or atom in the planes of matter. Therefore humans who are open to cosmic sight and divine understanding are able to activate these virtues and divine qualities in those places they are not experienced.

Free-will and conscious choice is a human super-power. Through deliberate conscious intent, an empowered human may direct Source Energy to manifest into form.

KEEPERS OF THE FLAME.

Co-Creating the Divine Plan, Heaven on Earth.

Activating, Manifesting, and Anchoring the Divinely Intended Plan is possible through The Power of the Spoken Word when aligned with Divine Will and the Sacred Heart. Each activation and integration of a divinely intended quality or virtue of the Ray Qualities increases the light quotient of the individual. This strengthens the Antakarana building the Rainbow Bridge and activates the Star Merkaba or Sacred Heart Torus.

The 12 Cosmic Rays as a list of Divine Virtue's or Qualities can be activated in the self and the world thus, seeding the new energies needed for the Ascension of Mother Earth. The human being is the mid-wife birthing the Golden Age of Enlightenment. When the human Invokes, Spirit Evokes. This means that by Placing ones hand on the sacred heart and speaking these affirmations out loud, the Higher Self will begin to Put Down these frequencies and fulfill each sacred decree declared.

12 SOLAR ASPECTS OF DEITY. Paths of Mastery

Ray 1, Sapphire Blue., Divine Will, Illuminated Faith, Power, Protection, God's First Cause of Perfection.

Ray 2, Sunshine Yellow. Enlightenment, Wisdom, Illumination, Understanding, Perception and Constancy.

Ray 3, Crystalline Pink. Transfiguring Divine Love, Adoration, Reverence for ALL Life and Tolerance.

Ray 4, White Sacred Fire. Ascension Flame, the Immaculate Concept, Purity, Restoration, and Resurrection.

Ray 5, Emerald Green. Illuminated Truth, Healing, Consecration, Concentration, and Inner Vision.

Ray 6, Ruby-Gold. Divine Grace, Healing, Devotional Worship, and Ministration of the Christo's

Ray 7, Violet. Freedom, Liberty, Justice, Victory, Mercy, Compassion, Forgiveness, and Transmutation.

Ray 8, Aquamarine. Clarity, Divine Perception, and Discernment.

Ray 9, Magenta. Harmony, Balance, Assurance, confidence.

Ray 10, Gold. Eternal Peace, Prosperity, Abundance, and Divine Supply of ALL good things.

Ray 11, Peach. Divine Purpose, Enthusiasm, and Joy.

Ray 12, Opal. Transformation and Transfiguration.

LIGHT ACTIVATION. Place hand on sacred heart and speak each divine virtue as an affirmation to activate, anchor and manifest the divine virtue in everyday form.

Ray 1, Divine Will, Illuminated Faith, Power, Protection, God's First Cause of Perfection.

I am the Will of God. The Will of God resides in me and my life.

I am aligned with Divine Will. Gods will works in and through me and my life. Not my will Gods Will works here.

I am the power of God. The Power of God is activated in me and my life. The Power of God resides in me and my life. I am Gods Power.

I am the Purpose of God. Gods Purpose is activated in me and life. Gods Purpose resides in me and my life.

I am the peace of God. The Peace of God is activated in me and my life. The Peace of God resides in me and my life.

I am the perfection of God. God perfection in activated in me and my life. God perfection resides in me and my life.

I am protected by God. Gods Protection is activated in me and my life. Gods Protection resides in me and my Life.

Ray 2, Love, Wisdom, Understanding, Beauty, Enlightenment, Illumination.

I am the Love of God. The Love of God resides in me. God love is activated in me and my life. God Love resides in me and my life.

I am the Wisdom of God. The wisdom of god resides in me. Gods wisdom is activated in me and my life.

I am the Understanding of God. The understanding of god resides in me. Gods Understanding is now activated in me and in my life.

I am the Beauty of God. Gods Beauty is activated in me and my life. Gods Beauty now resides in me and my life.

I am the Enlightenment of God. The enlightenment of god is now activated in me and in my life. Gods enlightenment now resides in me and my life.

I am the illumination of God. The illumination of God is now activated in me and my life. The illumination of god now resides me and my life.

Ray 3, Eternal Transfiguring Love, Creative Active Intelligence. Reverence for ALL Life and Tolerance.

I am the Love of God. The Love of god resides in me. The Love of God is now activated in me and my life. The Love of God now resides in me and my life.

Eternal Transfiguring Love is now activated in me and my life.

I am the intelligence of God. The intelligence of God is now activated in me and my live. The intelligence of God now resides in me and my life.

I am the creation of God I am as God Created me. The creation of God is activated ibn me and my life. The creation of God now resides in my life.

I am the action of God. The action of God is now activated in me and my life. The action of God now resides in me and my life.

I am the reverence of God. The reverence of god is now activated in me and my life. The reverence of god is now activated in me and my life.

Ray 4, Harmony, Purity, Restoration, Resurrection, Ascension Flame.

I am the harmony of God. The harmony of God is now activated in me and my life. The harmony of God now resides in me and my life.

I am the Purity of God. The Purity of God is now activated in me and my life. The purity of God now resides in me and my life.

I am the Restoration of God. The Restoration of God is now activated in me and my life. The restoration of God now resides in me and my life.

I am the Resurrection of God. The Resurrection of God is now activated in me and my life. The Resurrection of God is now activated in me and my life.

I am Ascended. The ascension of god is activated in me and my life. The ascension of god now resides in me and my life.

I am the Light of God. The Light of God is now activated in me and my life. The light of god now resides in me and my life.

I am the fire of god. The fire of god is now activated in me and my life. The fire of god resides in me and my life. The flame of god now burns through me and my life.

196

Ray 5, Truth, Healing, Concentration, and Inner Vision, Divine Intended Plan.

I am the Truth of God. The Truth of god is now activated in me and my life. The Truth of God resides in me and my life.

I am the healing of god. The healing of god is now activated in me and my life. The healing of god now resides in me and my life.

I am the concentration of god. The concentration of God is activated in me and my life. The concentration of God now resides in me and my life.

I am the vision of god. The Vision of God is activated in me and my life. The vision of God now resides in me and my life.

I am the divinely intended of god. Gods divine intentions are activated in me and my life. Gods divine intentions now reside in me and my life.

Ray 6, Divine Grace, Ministration of the Christo's. Peace and Good Will. Divine Brotherhood and Sisterhood.

I am the Grace of God. The grace of god is activated in me and my life. The grace of god now resides in me and my life.

I am the minister of god. God Divine Ministry is now activated in me and my life. Gods divine ministry is now activated in me and my life.

I am the peace of god. The peace of god is now activated in me and my life. The peace of god now resides in me and my life.

I am the good will of god. The goodwill of god is now activated in me and my life. The goodwill of god now resides in me and my life.

Gods Divine Brotherhood and Sisterhood is now activated in me and my life. Gods divinely intended brotherhood and sisterhood now resides in me and my life. I am the divinely intended brother and sister of life.

Ray 7, Freedom, Liberty, Justice, Victory, Mercy, Compassion, Forgiveness, and Transmutation. Ritual.

I am the freedom of god. The freedom of god is now activated in me and my life. The freedom of god now resides in me and my life.

I am the liberation of god. The liberation of god is now activated in me and my life. The liberation of god now resides in me and my life.

I am the justice of god. The justice of god is now activated in me and my life. The justice of god now resides in me and my life.

I am the mercy of god. The mercy of god is now activated in me and my life. The mercy of god now resides in me and my life.

I am the compassion of god. The compassion of god is now activated in me and my life. The compassion of god now resides in me and my life.

I am the forgiveness of god. The forgiveness of god is now activated in me and my life. The forgiveness of god now resides in me and my life.

I am the transmutation of god. The transmutation of god is now activated in me and my life. The transmutation of god now resides in me and my life. T

I am the ritual of god. The ritual of god is now activated in me and my life. The ritual of god now resides in me and my life.

Ray 8, Clarity, Divine Perception, and Discernment.

I am the clarity of god. The clarity of god is now activated in me and my life. The clarity of god now resides in me and my life.

I am the divine perception of god. The divine perception of god is now activated in me and my life. The divine perception of god is now activated in me and my life.

I am the discernment of god. The discernment of god is now activated in me and my life. The discernment of god now resides in me and my life.

Ray 9, Balance, Assurance, confidence.

I am the balance of god. The balance of god is now activated in me and my life. The balance of god now resided in me and my life.

I am the assurance of god. The assurance of god is now activated in me and my life. The assurance of god now resides in me and my life.

I am the confidence of god. The confidence of god is now activated in me and my life. The confidence of god now resides in me and my life.

Ray 10, Golden Way, Prosperity, Abundance, and Divine Supply of ALL good things.

I am the prosperity of god. The prosperity of god is now activated in me and my life. The prosperity of god now resides in me and my life.

I am the abundance of god. The abundance of god is now activated in me and my life. The abundance of god now resides in me and my life.

I am the divine supply of god. The divine supply of god is now activated in me and my life. The divine supply of god now resides in me and my life.

I am gods good. All gods good things are now activated in me and my life. All gods good substance now reside in me and my life.

I am the golden way of god. Gods golden way is now activated in me and my life. Gods golden way now resides in me and my life.

Ray 11, Divine Purpose, Enthusiasm, and Joy.

I am the divine purpose of god. The divine purpose of god is now activated in me and my life. The divine purpose of god now resides in me and my life.

I am the Joy of god. The joy of god is now activated in me and my life. The joy of god now resides in me and my life.

I am the enthusiasm of god. The enthusiasm of god is now activated in me and my life. The enthusiasm now resides in me and my life.

Ray 12, Transformation and Transfiguration.

I am the transfiguration of god. The transfiguration of god is now activated in me and my life. The transfiguration of god now resides in me and my life.

I am the transformation of god. The transformation of god is now activated in me and my life. The transformation of god now resides in me and my life.

ONE LIGHT AS A RAINBOW OF DIVINE GUIDANCE: Rainbow Bridge, (Spiritualization of Matter) ONE LOVE as unified Mind, Heart, and Body. The Christ Human, Ascended Master, is the inventor, engineer, executer, and progenitor of Source as the rainbow bridge unifying spirit and matter. Awakened Conscious Cosmic Angels now Free to Fulfill the Divine Plan as Eternal Souls in temporary human forms, with the Power, Love and Wisdom of God, as God. I AM THAT I AM.

COSMIC CONSCIOUSNESS.

THIRTEEN. Transcending 12 Dimensional Earth as MAGICAL BEING in the Number 13.

The number thirteen has been considered superstiscious in western society. The number 13 has been ommitted from most buildings. These buildings skip the thirteenth floor as if it does not exhist calling this floor the fourteenth floor.

In past life clearings more than one session came into the realization that their "immortal essence or divine knowing" was stolen from them and hidden up their colume of light at the 373rd level. This number, 373 adds up to thirteen. I believe the number thirteen was hidden from humans to keep humans blind and unaware of their inhierent birthrights and cosmic heritage as MAGICAL Co-Creator Beings with the Divine Mission or Sacred Purpose to Co-Create Heaven on Earth, Easily, Justly and for Being. (Being is the individuals resonant frequency or light quotient)

The number 13 is the Death Card of the Major Arcana of the Tarot. It is in the Archtype of the Four with the Emperor being the 4 of the Major Arcana. This is the foundation of global consciousness where humans enter into fulfilling life through Divine Fellowship, lifting each other up in Divine Reverence as Life, and Sacred Source. In Cosmic Consciousness the being remembers multiple lifetimes and recognizes the repetative patterns played out with other soul mates for many eons. (our brothers and sisters) Here Death is no longer the ending of the relationship, it is only a transition and opportunity to choose the next soul experience. A perception of Sacred Regerneration. The individual evolves from the soul experience of being bound to planet earth, and death into the experience of eternal Cosmic Consciousness.

Thirteen transcends the 12 Cosmic Rays of the Solar Heiarchy. This transcendance is Stepping off of the Wheel of Karma. Originally humans were intended to ascend and descend in life carnations by choice and free-will. The thirteen is a doorway or portal into the conscious awarenss of knowing that one is an omni-aware being with unlimited potential. This awareness is a natural process of ascension and of the increased frequencies of Mother Earth, our Galaxy and Universe. As Earth is now in the photon band, a high vibration field of light, that our galaxy is now spiraling through.

Humans are now not only remembering their past human lifetimes, they are also remembering past animal, plant, mythological, star-brother or sister and angel lifetimes. These memories are stored in the akashic records held in the DNA of cells. Some individuals even share that they are from the future. The archtypal pattern of energy is the same through each individual yet, the soul experience is unique for each individual. Perception is the key and easily changed through free-will and conscious choice. Each soul is infinite and eternal.

The experience of incarnating into life form on Planet Earth also carries the experience of death and birth. The perception that birth is painful and traumatic carries the soul wound of all new beginnings being painful and traumatic. The perception that death stops the individual from living carries with it a wound of limitation. The perception that life is a struggle, limiting, painful and against the self is another soul wound. The perception that death frees the person from painful life is also a deep soul wound. These perceptions keep the individual from knowing the inhierant truth of being an eternal soul in a temporary human form. These soul wounds are sometimes experienced as *Un-Healable Wounds, or Unforgivable Sins.* They are repeated through multiple incarnations and may be identified as curses and mortal wounds. At this crossroad the individual may experience a great amount of anxt and an increased desire to not be alive or in human form anymore. Bringing up all the wounds of suicide or suicidal ideation.

When the soul begins to be conscious of all are one and everyone is a reflection of the self as source, life may seem purposless. Yet everything *Matters*, every thought, feeling, action and perception is a vibrational frequency, and is directly creating the outer world or matter known as form that humans experience. The Spiritualization of Matter is the process of recognizing all life as sacred and the soul purpose to out-picture and fullfill the Divine Plan through conscious free-will and choice.

In truth each individual is an extention of us/one. Therefore the easiest way to fully co-create Heaven on Earth is to do so as a free soviergn individualized being with direct access to source energy. A shift from the unconscious parasitic energetics to a symbiotic consciousness of equal exchange. Fully disentangled from others psychic energy and collective entrainment. Choosing to join other free soviergen individuals in group prayer, intent, mantra, meditation and light activations of the Divinely Intended Plan.

The twelve cosmic rays or archtypes of the Solar Heiarchy are displayed on a wheel. While a circle is the symbol of wholness it is also a symbol of completion. The spiral allows the individual to spiral up above or down and opens the awareness of seeing the larger picture. This may be referred to as the "Single Eye of God" or Eagle Medicine. The ability to see the souls journey from a higher perspective. The eagle, pheonix and other winged animals are all representatives of a higher consciousness.

From these higher perspectives the individual becomes aware of the illusionary nature of earth life and the incredible gift of free-will and choice to liberate the self and Mother Earth. By Being in service to ones fellow brothers, sisters and Divine Mother/Matter the physical chalace of Life Source, through Heart Centered Knowing, through Co-Creating the intended, and Living Fully as Source. ONE LOVE.

MAGICAL BEING,

The individual can choose to experience the completion of all struggle and pain. They may also choose to experience the completion of Joyful Life, Sacred Purpose and Heaven on Earth.

Just for Being.....Meaning the outer world of form is manifested and created through the state of being or current resonant frequencies that are aligned with divine will and the divinely intended plan.

> *"Thank you God, Thank you Higher-Self for this (fill in blank) Divinely Intended Life, with Ease and Just for Being."*

Now fill in the blank with eveything and anything that is intended for Heaven on Earth, add momentum, feel the experience as if already happening, in gratitude, Sit back and be open to receive it in physical form.

Cosmic Consciousness of Magical Being.

ALL ARE ONE.

"Through the Power of the ONE Universal Truth, the ONE Heat, the One Unified Chrystoline Christ Consciousness in me".

Outer life is a reflection of inner programming, the current resonant frequency of self. Perception Shift. Raise or change the current vibrational frequencies and experience a change in outer life. The feeling is the key for frequency. "To feel as if, in the now".

> *"Thank you Higher-Self, Thank you God, for this chosen experience in the Now, Easily and Just for Being."*

> *"I claim my Divine Birthright to Manifest from thin-air into Physical Form, this sacred intention, Easily in the Now and Just for Being."*

Truth and God Knowing is with-in. As an Omni-Aware Being, Divine Knowing resides with-in the ascension chamber of the Sacred Heart. When the individual needs to know truth, place one hand on the sacred-heart and ask the higher self to reveal the answer or truth. The answer is returned through the language of the soul in symbol, metaphor, coincidance and multiple repetative signs.

> *"I claim my Divine Birthright to Know Truth, Have Truth, and Share Truth, Freely Easily and Safely, Just for Being."*

The Body/Matter is the container of sacred life. The human body is the sacred vessel of life. The vital life source is quickened, activated and restored in the body as the frequency and light quotient increase. The lower bodies control the vital life force essence. As the light body descends into to lower chakras it purifys each gland and chakra. This allows the electromagnetic kundalini vital life source from earth-source to ascend up the chakras restoring the fullness of the "divinely intended life" as health, vitality and inmortality. Moving from individual from the soul from being bound to the "death wounds" into the experience of freedom, liberation and "Fullfilling Life".

> *"I claim my Divine Birthright to fully restore the life force of vitality, health, well-being and inmortality in every cell of my body, Easily and Just for Being."*

> *"I claim Miraculous Healing as my Divine Birthright, Easily and Just for Being."*

Life is Sacred. Death is Sacred.

> *"I claim my Divine Birthright and take back my Divinely Intended Power to Give Birth to New Forms Freely, Easily and Safely, Just for Being."*

> *"I claim my Divine Birthright to Live Fully and Freely through Joy, Choice and Dignity, Easily, Just for Being."*

> *"I claim my Divine Birthright to Die through Freedom, Choice, Dignity and Joy, Easily, Just for Being. Today and Everyday."*

Super-Powers of the Avatar, Buddah or Christ are awakended, activated and miracles may be performed or experienced.

> *"I claim my divnely intended Super-Powers as an Unlimited Being, Easily, freely, safely and Just for Being."*

> *"I Claim my Divinely Intended Miraculous Experiences, Abilitities and Super-Powers, with Ease ad Just for Being."*

AFFIRIMATIONS OF INFINITE SUPPLY FOR THE GOLDEN AGE OF ENLIGHTENMENT

Place your hand on your Sacred Heart and Decree Out Loud through the Power of the Spoken Word.

Through the POWER OF THE ONE, UNIFIED HEART, the ONE UNIVERSAL TRUTH and the CHRIST IN ME:

I Claim my Highest Divinely Intended PURIFIED, FREE, SORVIERGN, UNLIMITED, INFINITE, ETERNAL, COSMIC, MULTI-DIMENSIONAL, MAGICAL BEING in physical and energetic form, In the Now with ease, Inherently just for being!

I Claim the Golden Age of Enlightenment is now activated in me and my life. I Claim my Golden Heritage. I Claim my Golden Way. I Claim my Golden Birthrights.

I Claim my Infinite Golden Potential as an Unlimited Being in temporary human form.

I Claim my Birthright to Remember my Original Souls; Origins, Purpose, Mission, Contracts, Lessons, and Intentions. I Claim my Birthright to Remember to Remember.

I Declare that my Original Souls; Origins, Purpose, Mission, Contracts, Lessons, and Intentions are NOW COMPLETE, FULFILLED, DONE and FINISHED. ALL is Finalized! I take my Divinely Intended Power to CHOOSE AGAIN, I Now only Choose through my conscious Free-Will, Joy and Choice!

I CHOOSE AGAIN... I Choose to co-create the New Earth, Heaven on Earth Now!

I Command my Pineal Gland and Pituitary Gland to stop producing death and decay hormones! I Command these Glands to begin to produce YOUTH and VITALITY HORMONES of immortality and for these youth and vitality chromosomes to be activated in my pineal gland, pituitary gland, every gland, every cell, molecule, DNA, RNA and Atom of my Being.

I Command my Pineal Gland and Pituitary Gland to vibrate simultaneously and rhythmically with my heart beat, the heartbeat of the earth and the heartbeat of the solar sun.

I Claim my Cosmic Sight! I take back my Power to See the Divinely Intended Beauty and Order in Everywhere, Everyone, and Everything!

I take back my power to embrace the Fullness of Life and to have the Fullness of Life Embrace me. I embrace Unconditional Love, Love embraces me. I embrace truth, truth embraces me. I embrace peace, peace embraces me.

I Claim the power of the 13 be restored as my Magical Birthrights! Three Magical Birthrights are:

I Claim Divine Revelation, my Divine Ability to KNOW Truth, HAVE Truth, and REVEAL Truth, Freely, Effortlessly and Safely, with Ease Just for Being!

I Claim Instant Manifestation, my Divine Ability to Manifest from "thin air/spirit" into physical Form all our needs and everything that provides or supports our Highest Good, Freely and Safely with Ease Just for Being!

I Claim Miraculous Healing my Divine Ability to Activate, Restore, Resurrect or Transfigure, the Divine Life Force in life captivated by the illusion of inertia, death and disease.

The Divine Life-force is now activated in me and my life.

The Ruby Red Ray of the Divine Life-force Force now rolls out ahead of me like the red carpet. Every step I take, Mother Earth and Father Spirit lift up all that Nourishes, Heals, Energizes, Motivates, Supports, Sustains and Provides for my Highest Good, with ease just for being.

I Claim my Super-Powers! I Claim my Cosmic Consciousness, my Cosmic Being, my Immortality, my Infinite Eternal Being.

I ask my Superpowers to be made KNOWN to me through my own personal God-Goddess Understanding and Sacred-heart. I Ask these be Physically Demonstrated and made known to me with ease, Just for Being. I Ask that these Super-Powers be DOWN-LOADED and ACTIVATED in my MULTI-DIMENSIONAL, DNA, IN THE NOW!

I Command my Solar Light Body to Activate and Anchor the maximum amount of Light intended for my Being continuously and with ease now. I Command my Star Merkaba to Activate and Spin now.

I AM a Crystalline Being. Christ Consciousness is activated in me and my life Now.

I AM an Eternal Being in temporary human form with Dominion, Free Will, and Unlimited Source within to Co-Create and Restore the Divine Plan of Heaven on Earth, today and every day, With Ease, Just for Being!

The Dream is Complete, Fulfilled and Whole. The Sacred Plan is Fulfilled Now.

Heaven is restored on Earth in the Now, with Ease, Just For Being!

LIGHT, LIGHT, LIGHT, Light is Produced at the Center of my Bones. Light, now bursts forth from the center of every atom of my multi-dimensional being. I Radiate Light, I Emanate Light, and I Illuminate Light. LIGHT, LIGJT, LIGHT, I AM LIGHT.

CHAPTER 6

―――――◉―――――

MASTER BEING

Easy Golden Age Play-Book. "Heaven on Earth, With Ease, Just for Being"

"All is intended to happen through prayer, Invocation, affirmation, claiming, and requesting or asking source from the sacred heart. And it does so due to our Inherent Value as divine sacred worthy and imperfectly perfect Co-Creator Being's. Ask and it will manifest in form.... JUST FOR BEING!!!"

The Golden Age of Life has a new Play-Book.

In the higher realms of conscious living the individual has gained some self-mastery and is now experiencing life that is supportive and conspiring to provide for the multi-dimensional self in the process of co-creating Heavenly Life. The Golden Age of Enlightenment, emerging as Crystalline Christ Consciousness.

I like to call this the process of Master Being. Master your life or your life will master you. The seventh ray is the ray of mastery, ritual and transmutation. Rituals may be referred to as the "Daily Self-Care Routines" for gaining self-mastery as a Master Being. Humans are intended to be Ascended Masters co-creating in accompaniment with the Spiritual Hierarchies.

Daily Routines are essential for self-mastery. The human mind must be trained to be continually conscious, 24/7, daily and continuously. As the Higher-self is placed in control (in the driver's seat) of the individual, the being begins to gain control and infinite power to co-create easily and immediately. With each heart-centered invocation of divinely ordered life the Higher-Self continues to evoke, putting down and delivering the matched frequency or physical equivalent in form. The momentum of divinely ordered live increases restoring the fullness of the intended life force. Life conspires to support and provided for every divinely intended need in all dimensions of human being. Mother Earth loves to respond through the elemental being's by providing and forming each sacred desire with ease. Life is teeming with abundance and bounty for all those who choose to co-create in the fullness of life.

Heaven on Earth is a living process. Manifestation is a living process. The human is the vessel of Source a conduit for divine expression of sacred life. The human is NOT separate from source. Source is Omni-Present. Human mind is a cognitive faculty allowing source to experience separation, individuation, relationship and transcendence of duality. Separation from God is the human's original soul wound. Source is with-in, with-out and ever present. Human mind is not source, human mind is the computer screen ready to deliver the answer asked from the sacred-heart. The sacred-heart is the portal for source to reside within, and respond from without. Sacred connection and belonging as one unified with the eternal sacred-heart of Source is an inherent right for humans.

The human mind of knowing of self as source is minimized like looking through a telescope lens. The Sacred-Heart unifies the multidimensional human mind, emotions and body. Transcending duality into sacred awareness of being an eternal soul in a temporary form, while carrying within the DNA the records or memories of infinite life forms. The "omni records" records of all knowing. An Omni-Present Infinite field of experiences and possibilities are held in the sacred white-fire center of every atom. Including with-in the human vessel.

Consciousness is the cause and substance of the human experience and perception. Consciousness is a field of unlimited potentials, while time equals a range of possibilities or experiences. Faith is the state of mind that can (envision, out-picture, imagine, visualize) see it as done. Belief is the feeling that re-programs the subconscious mind as feelings imprint the field of consciousness. The control of the subconscious mind is accomplished through control of conscious feelings. As Dr. Greg Braden says "The feeling is the prayer". When thoughts, feelings and body are aligned, the magical experience of manifestation happens. The experience of Heaven on Earth, Just for Being is first conceptualized then claimed or invoked and finally experienced or perceived as the current manifested reality. A living process co-creating hand in hand with source and as source. Divine Intelligence, Divine Understanding, Unconditional Love, and the Divine Power to choose One-Love as One-Heart-Beat is a conscious choice awakened in quickening of frequencies from with-in and with-out as the evolutionary Golden Age of Enlightenment. A prophecy foretold for millennia through countless cultures, philosophies, religions, artifacts, and the sacred-heart knowing of each atom and individual.

Daily Plays for an Enlightening Life of Heaven on Earth. With Ease, Just for Being.

1. **Your Divine Power;** Humans have inherent spiritual birthrights, qualities and virtues. **Inherent** implies our sacred divinity and rights are **Just for Being**, not for doing. **"Em-Power-Ment". Em**, is to Embody, the reception of divinity and co-creative abilities. **Power**, is I AM, Being God Goddess in human form. **Ment**, is Intent, the action of the divinity through conscious choice. Co-Creator beings are intended to fulfill the Divine Plan of Heaven on Earth.

   Choose Free-Will from this day forward. **Make a personal proclamation of one's own divinity as a sacred being who has value inherently.**

   Example...............

   Through the Power of the One Unified Crystalline Christ Heart in Me.

I _____(name) Now Proclaim I am Free! I Claim Free-Will as my Inherent birthright and one and only reality from this_____(date) day forward. I Claim I am Worthy and Valuable and_____(fill in blank) Just for Being! I now Choose _____(fill in blank) as my inherent right and reality, just for being. From this day forward I only draw into my life _____(fill in the blank) with ease and just for being. I Declare my right to experience relationships that are _____(fill in Blank) easily and just for being. I thank my Higher-Self and God for doing this for me.

Sign_____Date_____

2. **Activate Divine Understanding in the Sacred-Heart.** Invite Higher-Self to reside in the Heart from this moment forward and for the Higher-Self to guide oneself through one's own sacred-heart knowing and human understanding. Remember the soul's language is symbolism, synchronicity metaphor and coincidence. Be open to allowing the self to be as intended to be. *"I AM as God created me to be."*

   Example..........Place your hand on your heart, then speak OUTLOUD. *"My Higher-Self now resides in me. Divine Understanding is now activated in me. I Claim my birthright to KNOW, HEAR, and SEE as God Goddess, as Spirit does. I take back my power to Know, See and Hear as God & Goddess does, through my own Sacred Heart, my own Knowing and my own Understanding. I ask my Soul and Higher-Self to be with me today and always. I thank my Soul and Higher-Self for answering all my questions and for showing me my Divine Pathway. I ask this knowledge and guidance to be PHYSICALLY DEMONSTRATED, CLEARLY REVEALED, PLACED IN FRONT OF ME.*

Unify Sacred Heart and Sacred Mind through Sacred Embodiment. Place ones hand on the Sacred-Heart Space when asking the higher-self for guidance, during inner meditation and when one needs divine strength, balance, answers and peace.

Example of reminders for being heart centered and for remembering too place hand on heart when requesting divine guidance and proclaiming identified sacred-heart intended co-creation's are_____(Fill in Blank).

Be open to being Open Hearted, Ask Higher-self to remove any heart armor in an easy way.

3. **Ground Daily:** Ground 24/7 to the center of Earth and Sun. **Choose** to send ones roots to the center of the Earth-Heart and to the center of the sun's Solar-Heart. Invite or pull the energy up from earth-heart into one's own sacred-heart, and down from solar-heart into one's own sacred-heart. Unify one's heartbeat with the heartbeat of the earth and sun as One Heart Beat. This creates a strong column of light building the light strands of the **Rainbow Bridge** or Antakarana. It also activates the Solar Light Body the Chariot of Fire which is the natural form of an empowered human being. Acknowledge, Activate & Claim Unlimited Potential as an Eternal Being in Temporary Human Form. Build & Strengthen the Solar Light Body, Torus, Merkaba, and Column of Light through Light Affirmations. Be the Sacred White Fire at the center of each atom radiating light, as a Unified Sacred Heart Beat of ONE LOVE.

Create a meditation that is visual. Star Merkaba Meditations are examples of a visual meditation. One example is a you-tube video, named "12-D Shield Building Technique" by Energy Synthesis. Another is to imagine the self as a Tree with roots into the earth and leaves unified with the sunlight as the tree of life.

213

Visuals that support me in daily grounding are _____
Fill in Blank).

Create an oral meditation allowing the body to ground. Light Affirmations are examples of an oral meditation. *"Light, Light, Light, Light is Produced at the Center of my Bones. I Radiate Light, I Amplify Light, I Magnify Light, I Illuminate Light, I am Light, Light now Burst's forth from every Atom and Electron of my Being, I AM Light".*

Words, Sounds or Noises that support me in daily grounding are_____(fill in blank).

Create a daily physical routine adding a kinesthetic experience of grounding to the earth and solar heart as the rainbow bridge. Include the five senses as much as possible.

Examples include using essential oils for connecting and being one with the earth heart such as wood oils like white-fir, cedar-wood or patchouli. Use citrus oils for being one with the solar heart like grapefruit, orange or tangerine.

Another example is to physically reach down into the center of the earth with the right hand and pull energy from the earth-heart into one's own heart and then reach into the center of the sun with the left hand and pull energy from the solar-heart down into one's own heart while affirming the rainbow bridge is now complete.

Grounding technique's that may work for me are: _____
Fill in Blank).

Ask one Higher-self to reveal Angels, Elohim, and Animal Guides, Color, messages or other Divine Guidance through the soul's language of symbolism, for assistance in grounding to earth and the sun. Usually Angels are up the column of light and Elohim, Animal guides are down the column of light. This knowing is revealed through the sacred-heart when requested through inner meditation.

> Identified guidance for grounding and daily support is_____(fill in Blank)

Additional Grounding, It may be quite helpful to ground one's home, workplace, vehicle, painful body space and others spaces one resides to both the earth and sun heart. As this creates a free flow of Source Energy allowing each to become balanced and in harmony with the Divinely Intended.

> Identified places to ground to the Earth-Heart and Solar-Heart are: _____
> (fill in Blank).

4. **Practice daily Divine Detachment with Freedom & Sovereignty;** Claim Freedom and Sovereignty. Daily send all other people's energies, chords or psychic attachments home. Call home to self, one's own energy. **Claim direct access to Source Energy.** "Be the only thinker in your mind and the only feeler in your body". Tune into Inner truth and guidance with Divine Understanding of Source in your Sacred Heart. EARTH=HEART. The Ascension Chamber of ONE LOVE.

Freedom through Divine Detachment: Claim freedom and sovereignty daily. Once a day clear all other humans and non-human energies that may chord or attach to one of the causal bodies. Allowing for one to disentangle from the collective consciousness and freely manifest from the sacred heart as a free being.

> *"Through the power of the One Unified Heart and Crystalline Christ Consciousness in me, I claim freedom and SOVEREIGNTY as my inherent right and reality! Daily: I command all other people's energies, entities and archons to free and release me now. I thank my Higher Self and God for doing this for me.*

I claim Divine Detachment as my inherent right and reality. I now love all people and all people love me without attachment.

I Claim DIVINE DETATCHMENT as my Inherent Birth Right! I Command all archons, entities or other beings energies that are attached to me, feeding from me, draining me, chording me, inhibiting me or binding me, to FREE and RELEASE me now. Including all sexual attachments. You are no longer allowed to attach to any part of me. I send everyone else's energy home to them. I call back to me my own energy. I thank the angels and my Higher-Self for doing this for me in the Now.. I Now Love all people and all people Love me, without attachment."

I Am the only thinker in my mind and the only feeler in my body.

Remember everything in life is impersonal, when it is personal it is karmic. If it is karmic there is an opportunity to clear and transmute this karmic relationship through violet flame work.

5. **Set Daily Intent;** With Sound, Tone, Vibration & Frequency. Speak Into Form through positive language and affirmations as if happening in the Now. **Choice=Will**, Consciously Choose each Divinely Intended Idea through the Sacred Heart for the Divine Unified Good of ONE LOVE. "With Ease, Just for Being". **Deliberate Conscious Intent, choosing 24/7, Heavenly thoughts.**

   All Desires for co-creating or manifesting need to be aligned with one Highest Good in the Now. As Divinely Intended.

   Identify Sacred Intention from the Sacred Heart. The Divine Blue-Print, Highest Idea, or Possibility. These are the divinely intended qualities of the 12 Cosmic Rays.

Daily examples are: *I proclaim this day a Good Day!*

I claim success today and every day, I claim my divine good today and every day, I claim victory in this process.

I declare only divine order and harmony now work in me and my life. In work and my co-workers today.

Thank you God for the experience of_____ (fill in Blank) in the now, easily and just for being.

Identified Daily Intentions are?_____ (fill in Blank).

Daily affirmations and sacred intentions that will benefit me in the now are _____(fill in the blank).

Clear unconscious energetics blocking the sacred intent if needed. Ask Higher-Self through the On-Board Guidance System of the Sacred Heart if there are any unconscious energetics blocking the identified sacred intention.

Through the Sacred-Heart Knowing, (hand on hear and body pendulum) Locate the Body-Space or Chakra the energetic is stored or anchored in. Identify the unconscious emotions, thought forms, or mental agreements in the body space.

Sometimes it is helpful to use books such as Louis Hay's "You Can Heal You Life" or "Heal Your Body, The Metaphysical Causes For Physical Illness And The Metaphysical Way To Heal Them".

Ask Higher-Self to clear these energetic programs or blockages. Use the violet flame and choose the new reality in place of the old programming.

Clear the unconscious energetic that has been identified and clear through the process of Divine Revelation in Book Two of the Master Being Series.

Shift the 8 to the Infinite; Transcend Duality by shifting the 8 of heaven above earth, to the (Infinite, Infinity Sign), of Heaven beside Earth. **Be two people at once.** The person **experiencing the current reality** with love, compassion and forgiveness. The person **choosing to create the New Reality** as Divinely Intended. Acknowledge and invite every emotion into Love. For each undesirable experience, **choose Again,** Command and Ask Higher-Self, the Angels and Elementals to do the work for you. Ask for Sacred Desire from Sacred Heart and Let Spirit bring it into form for you. Magically Just for Being.

1. Identify current experience or reality. What are the thoughts and feelings I am having about myself, others or this situation?_____ (fill in Blank).

   Invite these emotions_____ into Love ask elementals to clear the records.

   Identify and Choose new thoughts as _____.
   Thank Higher-Self for activation and forward momentum of these new thoughts

2. What would I like to experience in this situation with myself, with others or in this situation? _____ (fill in Blank).

   I thank my Higher-Self and God for the experience of_____ (fill in Blank).

Pair every negative thought form with a positive affirmation or thought form as it happens.

NEW DAY, NEW WAY; This is the First time Humanity has an opportunity to Ascend as a Unified Family and in Relationship The

Blueprint or Sacred Script of this Paradigm, the Golden Age, is being written in the now, as each Human awakens to choose Love, Light, Truth and Peace in every moment through **BEING this vibration and frequency in form.** We are the Walking Christ's, we can heal ourselves, Our-Universe, in the now, with ease, **JUST FOR BEING.**

All mistakes are doorways to new choices and new opportunities. Each experience is an opportunity to assess its value for one's personal soul growth. Allowing empowerment, free-will and conscious choice to choose again thereby co-creating a new reality through the sacred science or manifestation and the power of the spoken word.

Co-creation is an active living process.

Identify conceived mistakes _____ (fill in Blank).

Identify how these have served the soul's process of awakening, becoming empowered and whole. _____ (fill in blank).

Choose new desired experience. _____ (fill in Blank)

Claim and activate these identified new experiences with the three fold conscious co-creation formula. _____. (fill in blank)

Cosmic Sight; Claim the Beauty Way, Take back divinely intended power to see, hear, and understand as Source does. See Divine Order and Beauty in everyone, everywhere and everything. **Envision Divine Good.** Ask for the Equivalent of Identified Good seen in others to be manifested as one's own Good in physical form. Create Vision Boards.

Be open to seeing the divinely intended in every situation. How would God see it?

Envision and imagine the desired goal, outcome through intention and out-picturing.

Create a Vision Board with visual images of desired intended good. Place a picture of self, God and Self having the desired goal in the vision board.

How does God or your Higher-Self see your life and what is divinely intended for self?

Identify _____ (Fill in Blank).

Original Innocence in Upgraded Form; Claim, download and activate one's Original Innocence and **SUPER-POWERS** in their Upgraded Form in the Now. The DNA Light Activation and Divine Alignment of Multi-Dimensional Being as Crystalline Consciousness of ONE-LOVE. **Sacred, Worthy and Valuable, Just for Being.**

I _____(name in blank) Claim my Original Innocence and ask it to be downloaded and fully activated in my DNA and every-day knowing in the now.

Upgraded Form: Continue to claim ones intended abilities and super-powers and ask these to be activated in the DNA in the Now. Identify_____ (fill in Blank).

Transmutation; As With-In, So With-Out. Identify undesirable experiences, obstacles and blockages. Place each into the Violet Fire of Purification. Clear the Multi-Dimensional Being of karma, spiritual contracts, vows and agreements through the individualized Crystalline Consciousness of One Unified Love in the Sacred Heart. Every experience in life is **In-Personal**, when it becomes personal it is Karmic. **Be the Alchemist turning each less than experience into the Intended Golden Potential.** "Rearranging the molecules right in front of my being, manifesting into form all of my dreams." I AM a Golden Being with Golden Potential.

Practice placing into the Violet Flame all undesired experiences. Use the power of the spoken word for this or write it out on paper. Burn if needed.

Chant Violet Flame Mantras for seven minutes a day.

Chant Shiva, Om Namyo Shivia, or other mantras for removing obstacles.

Personal examples and options for Violet Flame work _____ (fill in Blank).

Immaculate Concept; Hold the thought of purity and divinely intended good for and on behalf of self, loved ones, friends, family communities and life. Envision everyone and everything as whole, fulfilled and complete. **Speak into Form through the Power of the Spoken Word.** Thank Spirit for activation, restoration and fulfillment of each sacred decree in physical form.

Hold the highest idea for and on behalf of every part of life. Identify the negatives and begin to activate the Divine Ideas of the 12 cosmic rays in this situation, person, relationship or society.

ONLY LOVE IS REAL

EXAMPLE OF PERSONAL PROCLOMATION

AS ABOVE SO BELOW

Standing in my Divineity as My Higher Self, Through the Power of the ONE HEART and Crystalline Christ in me.

I _____ now declare, I AM a Sacred Co- Creator Being. From this day _____ forward, I claim my Divinity and my birth-right to create Heaven on Earth. From this day forward I Choose to Stand In My Light, to radiate and emanate my true light self wherever I journey. I claim Victory in this declaration!

I _____ now acknowledge my rightful divinity and connection with all beings divine. I AM never alone and now call on my higher-self, Angels, Guides, Elohim, and any other beings of light to assist me everyday and in everyway, for my highest good and the highest good of all my loved ones. I claim Victory in this declaration!

Whenever the density of human fear makes itself known to me, I now choose to listen, see, and love this fear as perfect. This fear has served me perfectly, by teaching me_____, and blessing me with_____. I invite this fear into love, for it has never known love. I call on all the angels, guides and elementals to now escort this fear into love, transmuting it to its higher form. Thank You Spirit, Thank You Self!! I claim Freedom, Liberation and Victory in this process!

From my higher-self, I now choose to allow forgiveness into my life wherever it most serves me. I do not have to know how to forgive; I must only be open to forgiveness for it to happen. I invite all my angels, and guides to assist me in receiving the **GRACE OF SPIRIT**, by forgiving myself and all others who have ever wronged me. Therefore I now am open too, and send my forgiveness wherever it is most needed. I claim Freedom, Liberation and Victory in this process!

From my higher-self, I now choose to begin an inner dialogue with my inner-selves. I choose to open a doorway of conversation with my inner-child, and inner-warrior. My higher-self now invites the inner-selves into a relationship of **Sacred Trust** until each comes together in embrace, balance and love. My higher-self acknowledges that each of the inner-selves is right, perfect and okay, yet my Higher-self is now in the 'driverseat', and gently guides each of the inner-selves into choosing what is now for the highest good. I utilize muscle testing if needed to make this decision. I claim Freedom, Liberation and Victory in this process!

From my Higher-self, I now begin to have conversations including verbal conversations with my physical vehicle/body. I thank my body for housing my spirit and soul. I thank my body for housing all of my multidimensional self. I only speak words and hold thoughts of love, kindness, and encouragement, to the physical body from here on out.

If I find myself holding a dense thought or statement, I immediately forgive this thought, and myself, and invite it into love. I then restate from my higher-self true thoughts of love and acceptance. I claim Freedom, Liberation and Victory in this process!

From my higher-self, I begin to have conversations with my cellular memories, RNA, and DNA, I give permission for each of these to be released of any misqualified energies, and now invite them to realign, restructure, and be brought forth into my highest divinely intended form. In this dialogue I Am aware that I am conversing with the elemental realm. I claim Freedom, Liberation and Victory in this process!

Standing in my Divinity, as my Higher-self, I now choose to hold thoughts of purity and love for and on behalf of family, my friends, mankind and myself. I choose to practice the act of the "IMMACULATE CONCEPT". (Requested by the QUEEN OF HEAVEN, channeled through CAMILLE)

GODS PERFECT LOVE NOW DOES ITS PERFECT WORK IN AND THROUGH _____.

ONLY LOVE WORKS IN AND THROUGH_____, IN AND THROUGH ME, AND IN AND THROUGH OUR RELATIONSHIP!

ONLY DIVINE ORDER EXHISTS IN_____, ONLY DIVINE ORDER EXHIST IN ME.

ONLY DIVINE ORDER WORKS IN_____, ONLY DIVINE ORDER WORKS IN ME, ONLY DIVINE ORER EXHISTS IN OUR RELATIONSHIP.

I Affirm:

THE HEALING LOVE OF GOD NOW FLOWS THROUGH ME
AND FLOWS THROUGH MY HANDS.

I BLESS MYSELF AND OTHERS WITH EVERYTHING I TOUCH.

I AM AS GOD CREATED ME.
I SEE AS GOD SEES.
I HEAR AS GOD HEARS.
I AM THE WORD OR GOD.

I AM THE LIGHT OF GOD.
I AM THE SOUND OF GOD.
I AM THE LOVE OF GOD.
I AM THE ACTION OF GOD.
I AM THE FULLFILLMENT OF GOD.
I AM MY GOD SELF TODAY.
I AM, I AM, I AM…..

OM……

Additional Notes: Continue to identify daily routines and practices that empower the self to stay grounded, open and ready to accept Divine Good in every aspect of life.

LIGHT ACTIVATION PLAY-SHEET

I PROCLAIM HEAVEN ON EARTH NOW!

**Place hand on Sacred Heart and speak out loud
through the power of the spoken word.**

THROUGH THE POWER OF THE ONE UNIFIED HEART, THE ONE UNIVERSAL TRUTH
AND THE CHRIST IN ME, I NOW INVOKE, ACTIVATE, RECOGNIZE AND COMMAND
THE DIVINE QUALITIES OF FREEDOM, JUSTICE, LIBERATION AND DIVINE
OPPORTUNITIES FOR ME, MY FAMILY, FRIENDS, COMMUNITY, WORLD, PLANET
EARTH, UNIVERSE, CELESTIAL REALM, ELEMENTAL REALM, AND ALL SENTIENT
BEINGS THROUGH ALL DIMENSIONS SPACE AND TIME.

THROUGH THE POWER OF THE ONE UNIFIED HEART, THE ONE UNIVERSAL TRUTH
AND THE CHRIST IN ME, I NOW COMMAND ALL SECRETS, BETRAYALS, HIDDEN
AGENDAS, MISINFORMATION, MISNOMERS, DECEPTION, LIES, COVER-UPS, FALSE
PRETENSES AND FAKE SITUATIONS TO BE CLEARLY REVEALED IN THE LIGHT, MADE
KNOWN, AWARE, RECOGNIZED AND CONSCIOUS TO ALL, AS IS FOR THE HIGHEST
GOOD! LIGHT, LIGHT, LIGHT ALL IS REVEALED THOUGH LIGHT NOW!

THROUGH THE POWER OF THE ONE UNIFIED HEART, THE ONE UNIVERSAL TRUTH
AND THE CHRIST IN ME, I NOW INVOKE, ACTIVATE, RECOGNIZE AND COMMAND
THE DIVINE QUALITIES OF RESURRECTION, PURIFICATION, TRANSFORMATION,
TRANSMUTATION AND RESTORATION TO NOW RESIDE AND WORK THROUGH ALL
LIFE INFINITELY AND ETERNALLY!

THROUGH THE POWER OF THE ONE UNIFIED HEART, THE ONE UNIVERSAL TRUTH
AND THE CHRIST IN ME, I COMMAND THE DIVINE LIFE SOURCE TO BE ACTIVATED,
RESTORED AND RESIDE IN THE HEARTS AND MINDS OF ALL SENTIENT BEINGS!
I DECLARE THE DIVINE LIFE SOURCE NOW MOTIVATES, ACTIVATES, ENERGIZES,
EMPOWERS, PROVIDES, NOURISHES, FEEDS, FULFILLS, SUSTAINS, SUPPORTS,
PROVIDES AND SERVES ME, EVERYWHERE, EVERYONE AND EVERYTHING
INCLUDING MOTHER EARTH AND ALL SENTIENT BEINGS!

THE POWER OF THE ONE UNIFIED HEART, THE ONE UNIVERSAL TRUTH, THE
CHRIST CONSCIOUSNESS, THE BUDDHA CONSCIOUSNESS AND INFINITE ETERNAL
AWARNESS OF LOVE ARE NOW ACTIVATED AND MANIFESTING THROUGH ALL
DIMENSIONS IN THE MINDS AND HEARTS OF ELEMENTAL, CELESTIAL, HUMAN

OR OTHER FORMS, VIBRATIONS AND ENERGIES INCLUDING ALL ASPECTS OF SITUATIONS, COUNTRIES, SYSTEMS, STRUCTURES, RULES, PEOPLE, LANDS, FAMILIES, ANIMALS, PLANTS, INSECTS AND OTHERS NAMED OR UNNAMED!

The Great Invocation

From the point of Light within the Mind of God

Let light stream forth into the minds of men

Let Light descend on Earth.

From the point of Love within the Heart of God

Let love stream forth into the hearts of men.

May Christ return to Earth.

From the center where the Will of God is known

Let purpose guide the little wills of men-

The purpose which the Masters know and serve.

From the center which we call the race of men

Let the Plan of Love and Light work out

And may it seal the door where evil dwells.

Let Light and Love and Power restore the Plan on Earth.

INVOKING LIGHT
I walk forth Straight, Tall, Clear.
Aligned with Divine Will & Might!
All in Life is Right... Standing in my Light.
Mighty I AM Presence Guide my Way... Letting Spirit Play today!
From my Sacred Heart, Joy & Bliss Now Start!
As a Star, Shining Bright.. All Freedom now takes Flight.
As I Claim my Sacred Being... Victory Reveals....
Only Love is Real! Only Love is Real!
As Above So Below, Heavenly Life, It Is So!
God & Goddess UNITE it is our Magic Rite!

Aligning Shining Star, 08-18-2010
Camille Moritz

ABOUT THE AUTHOR

Camille's Story:

Born an empath with intuitive and psychic knowing. I was raised on Lazy Mountain in the rich rural farmland of Palmer Alaska. The animals, trees, nature spirits and plants were my friends. I was taught transcendental meditation at the age of five and received valuable spiritual instruction from a family friend who was an Athabaskan Spiritualist. She taught me how to protect myself during nightly astral projections, by speaking the Lord's Prayer and calling my Higher- Self to lead me into the higher realms of angelic and celestial light

As I was often over-stimulated by intense intuitive awareness. I was instructed to intentionally visualize color and light around others for peaceful healing-love. This allowed me to shift the empathic experience of sensing their pain. Visualizing color around others was the most precious gift of self-empowerment and personal growth.

I had repetitive prophetic dreams about the "end of the world or the great shift" and my part to share wisdom in these times. Too further understand this inner knowing, I began reading Edger Casey at age 12 and anything else I could find in the esoteric arts. I began giving Tarot Readings and offered a mini informational class about Tarot to local ladies club at age 18. Despite these natural abilities I found personal human interaction to be overwhelming, challenging and even painful. I would often avoid groups and public gatherings. Seeking solace with animals, children and nature.

Enrolling in college to gain knowledge and wisdom for this inner guidance of sacred purpose. I went on to obtain a Bachelor's Degree in Psychology and Philosophy from the University of Alaska, Anchorage. Then enrolled in a specialized Graduate program in Jungian Archetypal and Body Centered Therapies. While jumping full on into family life, I raised three children and now have three grandchildren.

In service to Humanity and One Love, my career has always been in social service organizations. Spending time as activities therapist, residential counselor, correctional officer and clinical case manager of both children and adults in numerous settings. Implementing, coordinating, teaching and providing therapeutic services. Over time my higher-self's inner-urge to fulfill my soul's mission increased. Where I branched out to open a small Metaphysical Healing Center in Homer, Alaska.

I have had many visions, ascended masters, saints and guides come to speak with me through-out my life. During my own personal development, Divine Mother as Guadalupe pressed itself in my third-eye, for weeks she was in my sight with my eyes both open and closed. Divine Mother continues to guide, heal and speak through me in many forms. Her instruction and channeled guidance allowed me to down-load an in-depth transformational system of divine revelation whereby each soul is freed of karmic debt through revealing, clearing, transmuting, activating and manifesting the Divinely Intended Plan or Blueprint of Heaven on Earth.

Camille's Approach:

I have combined my traditional education and human services experience with my esoteric studies, alternative healing talents, and information that is received from Spirit through personal guidance and channeling sessions.

I believe that each person has a divine purpose for existence and is participating in a co-creative process with Spirit to find or explore this purpose. The co-creative process is both an individual and a collective process. Humans are creator beings whose overall purpose is to create Heaven on Earth. Each of us steps into our unique role as a co-creator by being our highest self on Earth. The first step in this process is to "Know thyself."

Spirit and soul language is the language of symbols, myths, and visions. Often people choose to be born into a family or an environment in which they can complete karmic work. Many of us have made past or current life agreements, contracts, or vows that keep us from living up to our current life potential. By being in touch with our inner or soul process, we can begin to unravel our own personal mysteries, move into awareness, and travel our unique path to source, nirvana, enlightenment, mastery, etc. It is from our divine or core self that we can once again feel connected to divine source and begin to fulfill our divine purpose in life.

Spiritual intuitive readings often validate an individual's current process or experience. Readings can help people find and erase limiting soul contracts or vows, thereby helping them return to an empowered state of joy. Readings also can help individuals get in touch with their guides, angels, and other spiritual helpers. Often during readings, people are able to make contact with loved ones who have passed to the world of spirit. Individuals sometimes also explore past life experiences during readings, integrating these into present life experience.

In-Depth Transformational clearing sessions allow the individual to identify and remove any obstacle that would keep one from fulfilling their Divine Purpose. This process identifies the soul's records and clears spiritual contracts or other energetics that would keep the soul bound to limitation. Crystal Light Activation sessions, utilize vibrational healing tools to support and clear the multidimensional human body of limitations, thus freeing and restoring the fullness of health, vitality and freedom. This is a life journey of self-mastery and service to One Unified Love.

Through spiritual development and a personal relationship with Higher-Self, Spirit, it brings me great joy to serve the One Unified Love. As a representative of the Divine Mother, the Celestial Elemental Realms, Councils of Record Keepers, and Unified Team-Light & Team-Dark. The Golden Age of Enlightenment is now and it is time to Awaken. Together we may walk the Golden Path of Eternal Peace, Love and Harmony. All are Sacred. All is Love.

ONLY LOVE IS REAL!

Camille Moritz, Revelator of Light

69263053R00147

Made in the USA
Lexington, KY
28 October 2017